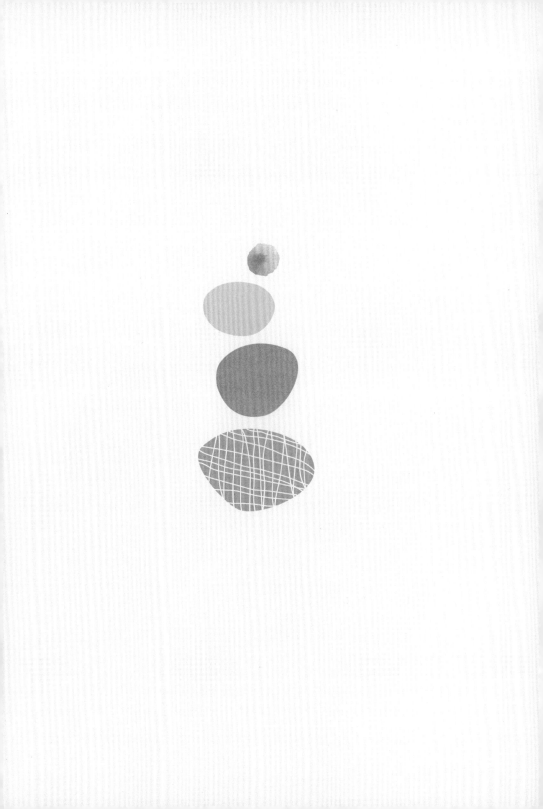

A
BEGINNER'S
GUIDE
TO

CHAKRAS

OPEN
THE
PATH
TO
POSITIVITY,
WELLNESS
AND
PURPOSE

LISA BUTTERWORTH
WITH PHOTOGRAPHY BY LISA LINDER

Smith
Street
Books

CONTENTS

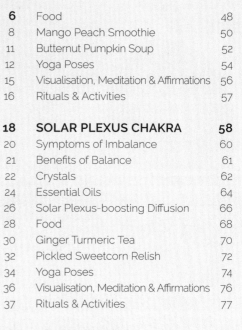

INTRODUCTION

Energy. It's all around us. It's within us. It *is* us. Tapping into energy, raising our awareness of its flow and effects, and learning how to clear, shift and activate it in our bodies is a crucial element of overall well-being.

If you have ever left a yoga class feeling incredibly open-hearted, or felt a zing in your third eye when you smelt a particular essential oil, or enjoyed the deep inner calm from a meditative experience, you know first-hand the incredible benefits of engaging with our energy centres, known as chakras. With roots in the spiritual texts of ancient India, the chakra system has evolved to be a modern-day tool for balance, self-care and radiant healing.

Tuning in to your chakras, understanding their energy and learning different ways of moving and enhancing them will add a whole new depth to your health, well-being and life in general. Working with the chakras is a journey of wellness, but it is also a path to immense love, happiness, purpose, compassion, spirituality and bliss. The following pages offer an introductory guide to this powerful system, including easy-to-understand breakdowns of what each chakra represents as well as a number of methods for working with each one. The information included here just begins to scratch the surface of this ancient system, and the incredible benefits engaging your energy centres can effect. Each of us is a being of light and energy; the chakras offer a pathway to transformation.

THE CHAKRA SYSTEM

Anyone who has taken a yoga class is probably familiar on a surface level with the concept of chakras. You may have a general understanding of their placement in the body. Or you might be aware of the vibrant rainbow of colour associated with the system. Or you may know nothing at all, in which case, welcome! You are in for a mind-expanding, heart-opening, soul-fortifying treat! Deepening our knowledge of the chakra system is the first step towards understanding how we can nourish and heal our chakras to bring a greater sense of happiness, purpose and peace to our lives.

WHAT ARE CHAKRAS?

Chakras are a system of energy centres in the body. Each one corresponds with different systems and organs within the body. The chakras also govern different mental and emotional aspects of our being. Many ancient cultures convey the belief of an energetic, chakra-like system that is tied to both health and enlightenment, but the chakra system we are familiar with in the Western world has its roots in India.

Chakra: In Sanskrit, *chakra* comes from the word *cakra* (pronounced with a 'ch'), which means spinning wheel.

A BRIEF HISTORY

The earliest mention of chakra comes in the Vedas, ancient Indian religious texts originating circa 1500 BCE that provide the foundation for Hinduism. The chakras were further explored in the Upanishads, sacred Hindu texts beginning in 800 BCE, which expound on the truths put forth by the Vedas. This is when chakras were given locations and symbolism. A later 10th century text written by master Hindu yogi Gorakhnath spoke of awakening and meditating on the chakras.

The texts that helped bring this system to the West were the 10th century's Padaka-Pancaka and the 16th century's Sat-Cakra-Nirupana (an exploration of the six centres). They were translated from Sanskrit by John Woodroffe, a Calcutta-born Brit, in his 1919 book *The Serpent Power: The Secrets of Tantric and Shaktic Yoga*, written under his pseudonym Arthur Avalon. Following texts helped solidify the seven-chakra system as interpreted by Western thought, as well as its association with the rainbow spectrum of colour.

Following modern interpretations and contemporary evolution, working with the chakra system has become less tied to a religion and more a practice for holistic healing and well-being.

Crown

Root

Third Eye

Sacral

Throat

Solar Plexus

Heart

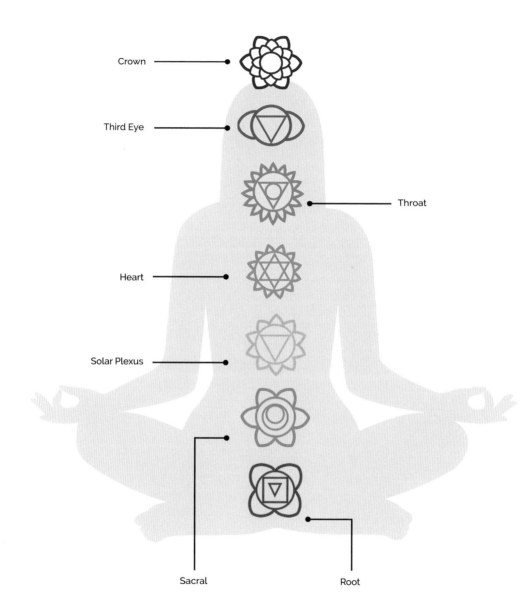

AN OVERVIEW OF THE CHAKRAS

Though the chakra system has included a number of different energy centres over its millennia of evolution, and even now includes many 'minor chakras', this book centres on the seven-chakra system.

THE SEVEN-CHAKRA SYSTEM

The chakras are located along the centre of the body, from the pelvic floor to the crown of the head. Each chakra corresponds with different elements or organs of the physical body and each one is associated with a colour, a symbol, a sense, an element and an affirmation. We will get into these in detail in the coming chapters, but here is an overview to get us started.

Root Chakra: The root chakra is the first of the energy centres, located at the pelvic floor. It governs our security and physical survival. It is the first of the three physical chakras.

Sacral Chakra: Moving up, the sacral chakra is our emotional centre, existing just below the navel.

Solar Plexus Chakra: Our solar plexus chakra regulates self-worth and empowerment. It sits just above the navel.

Heart Chakra: The heart chakra is all about love. It governs our relationships and resides in the centre of the chest. It is the bridge between the three lower physical chakras, and the three upper spiritual chakras.

Throat Chakra: This is our centre of communication and self-expression. It is located at the base of the throat, and acts as a doorway connecting us to the divine.

Third Eye Chakra: Located just between our brows, the third eye teaches us to truly 'see'. It governs our inner wisdom and intuition.

Crown Chakra: Located just above the crown of the head, this chakra is pure awareness and spirituality, the portal to a higher consciousness.

UNDERSTANDING ENERGY

To better understand the chakra system, it helps to get acquainted with the concept and science of energy, and how it can be viewed as we begin to engage and activate our body's energy centres.

THE PHYSICAL BODY & THE ENERGETIC BODY

The physical body is something we are all familiar with; we all recognise the biological systems and organs that keep our bodies breathing and moving. What we cannot see is our energetic body, also called the subtle body. The two are intricately connected, and the chakra system is our blueprint for understanding and healing our energetic body. Though Western medicine focuses almost entirely on the physical, a holistic vision of health and well-being must take into account our energetic body – the flow, the blockages, the vitality of the energy running through us. Bringing it into balance creates a state of harmony, boosting the health of body, mind and spirit.

WHAT IS ENERGY?

Everything is made up of energy. What's more, the amount of energy in the universe is a constant and can only be changed from one form to another. The energy of our subtle body can get stuck, cleared, depleted and enhanced, and this movement of energy can have far-reaching effects.

PRANA & PRANAYAMA

When we talk about energy in relation to the chakra system it is often referred to as *prana*, the Sanskrit word meaning 'life force'. Breath is a vital element of *prana*, carrying the life force into our bodies. In Sanskrit, *ayama* translates as 'to extend or draw out', and *pranayama* is the practice of controlling the breath.

A STATE OF FLOW

When our chakras are in harmony, each one spinning and humming with vibrant and balanced energy, *prana* flows seamlessly through our body. We are in good health, physically, mentally, emotionally and spiritually. But any number of things can affect our energy – life events, negative patterns, unprocessed emotions, self-critical thinking. It's all interconnected and can result in energy that's blocked (an underactive chakra) or energy that surges untempered (an overactive chakra). Engaging with your chakra system will give you insight into where your energy centres are out of alignment and how you can work towards bringing balance.

GETTING TO KNOW YOUR CHAKRAS

Engaging the chakra system and tuning in to your energetic body is a wonderfully nourishing practice. It will deepen your self-awareness, connect you to your body, your environment and your fellow humans, and will open you up spiritually as well. And it's fun! Here are a few things to keep in mind.

Start at the Root As you familiarise yourself with the symptoms of imbalance, you may feel like it is chakras other than your root that need attention. But starting at the root can ensure you have a good foundation of healing. When you are just getting acquainted with this powerful system, tending to your chakras in order can help you understand how the system as a whole works. Once you have worked to bring them into balance in order, it will be easier for you down the line to understand where the work is needed.

Consider It Self-care For those who are driven doers, getting the chakras aligned may feel like an extensive checklist of the soul, and you might be eager to start ticking off boxes. Instead, try to think of this as a gentle journey of exploration and discovery. The following chapters are full of ways to truly take care of yourself. Luxuriate in the process, have gratitude for the specific journey you are on, and try to hold space for the needs of each chakra whatever they may be and however long it might take.

Be Patient Getting to know our chakras and bringing them into balance can be quite a process. You might not make immediate progress, have life-changing breakthroughs or even have the space in your schedule for dedicating time to the endeavour. Don't get discouraged. Treat yourself with the love and kindness an open heart chakra inspires. Try to be patient and trust the journey. The path you are on is the right one.

Consider Outside Healing You may find that at some point in your chakra work, you come to a block that just won't budge. You may benefit from seeing an outside healer, someone certified and gifted in energy work, who can give your process a boost. There are lots of different types of energy work – from reiki and crystal healing to acupuncture and breathwork. Find the type that is best suited to you and your individual needs.

Each Chakra Is Different You may find that your root chakra feels almost effortlessly balanced, but that your heart chakra involves tons of time and practice to sort through its energetic layers. Not all your chakras will require the same amount of energy and attention. Remember that working with the chakras is an intuitive practice. Not every visualisation in this book will resonate with you, not every affirmation will be meaningful. That's OK. Take what works and learn from it. There is so much more to the chakra system and its methods of healing than this book could begin to hold. Your journey is just beginning!

HOW TO USE THIS BOOK

The following chapters are organised by chakra. Each one includes an overview of the chakra's energy as well as explanations of the manifestations of imbalance and the benefits of harmony. It also outlines a number of methods and suggestions for tuning in to, clearing and energising each particular chakra.

Crystals: Although crystals aren't a necessary element of chakra work, they can be helpful in connecting us with the energy we are trying to cultivate. Different crystals resonate with different chakras, and simply having them around and being mindful about their purpose can help us tap into the work we are doing.

Essential Oils: Like crystals, these oils aren't essential, but bringing their plant magic into your chakra practice can open things up in a whole new way. Many of the oils mentioned in this book can influence and support more than one chakra, so use your intuition. Essential oils can be irritating to the skin, so always blend them with a carrier oil, like sunflower, sweet almond or jojoba oil.

Food: 'Eating the rainbow' is one of the easiest ways to ensure you are getting the necessary nutrients across a spectrum of fruit and vegetables. It is also helpful when tending to the chakras, as each colour resonates with a different energy centre.

Yoga Poses: Yoga and the chakra system are related. Different poses, or *asanas*, can affect different chakras, helping to unblock energy centres, move stagnation and redistribute *prana* throughout the body. As you utilise the poses, listen to your body. Use the breath to deepen your poses safely, and modify when necessary. Inversions (including Plough Pose, Shoulderstand and Headstand) should not be practised during menstruation. Those with asthma should be mindful when practising breathwork.

Visualisation, Meditation, Affirmations & Ritual: The power of visualisation, meditation, affirmations and ritual cannot be overstated. They can harness the power the mind has on the physical and energetic bodies to great effect.

BE SMART ABOUT YOUR HEALTH

Although engaging the chakra system and working to bring all your energy centres into alignment can have wonderful benefits for your physical health, energy work is not the same as receiving medical attention. If you have any physical ailments or illnesses, you should utilise all of the wellness tools available to you, including medical physicians as well as holistic practitioners, to work in tandem with the practices you are cultivating at home.

ROOT CHAKRA

Stability ✦ Survival ✦ Security

Overview: The root chakra is the lowest chakra in our energetic system. It is the first of the physical chakras, grounding us to our earthly existence. Located at the base of the spine, it acts as an energetic foundation, which is why your chakra work should begin here. A healthy, balanced root chakra creates the foundation we need to align and open the chakras above it. Just as you wouldn't build a house on shifting sands, you don't want to work on balancing the upper chakras without clearing and connecting to your base chakra. If you think of your energetic system as a tree, the root chakra is just that – the strong, deep roots from which a big and beautiful tree can grow and thrive. Tending to our root chakra creates a strong energetic foundation that helps bring balance to our system as a whole.

Sanskrit Name

Muladhara: *Mula* means 'root', while *adhara* means 'support'.

The root or base chakra is all about security and stability. It is tied to our basic human needs of survival – food, water, shelter. Emotionally it fuels our sense of belonging. But, as one of the three chakras of matter, it also fuels how we feel in our body, and how our body feels on the planet. Not only does it govern our connection to the ground we walk on, but also the connection we have to our family, both blood and chosen. It is the energy that roots us in our system of security and support. Our confidence, trust and feelings of safety and belonging are all tied to *muladhara*. A healthy root chakra provides a confident stability, feelings of safety both physical and emotional, and helps us feel connected to nature, ourselves and one another. It is a grounding force, tethering us to the earth so that we can grow and our spirit can fly.

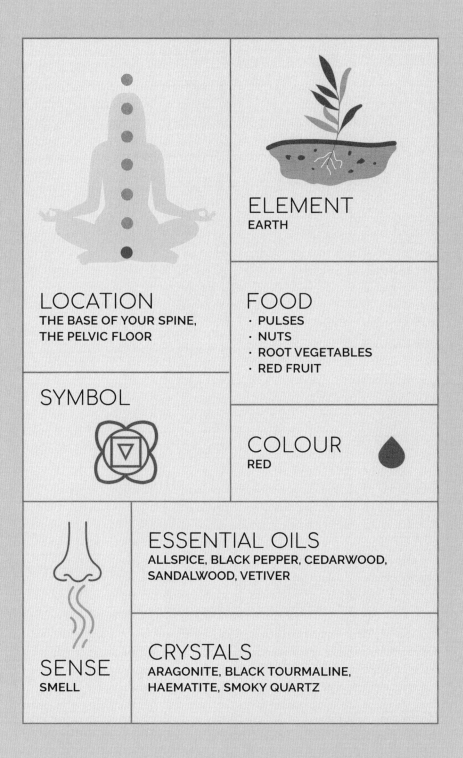

LOCATION
THE BASE OF YOUR SPINE,
THE PELVIC FLOOR

SYMBOL

ELEMENT
EARTH

FOOD
· PULSES
· NUTS
· ROOT VEGETABLES
· RED FRUIT

COLOUR
RED

ESSENTIAL OILS
ALLSPICE, BLACK PEPPER, CEDARWOOD,
SANDALWOOD, VETIVER

CRYSTALS
ARAGONITE, BLACK TOURMALINE,
HAEMATITE, SMOKY QUARTZ

SENSE
SMELL

SYMPTOMS OF IMBALANCE

When our root chakra is out of balance, it can affect us both mentally and physically. And because it plays such an important role, acting as an energetic foundation, these effects can ripple throughout our being.

Overactive Chakra: If you think of *muladhara* as a root system, it is easy to understand the types of issues that can arise. An overactive root chakra can create stagnation, a detrimental resistance to change. It can manifest as overattachment to the physical world and its material goods or an unhealthy indulgence in food or sex.

Underactive Chakra: When our root chakra is underactive, it can create heightened feelings of fear and insecurity. We may feel disconnected not only from the earth, but from those around us as well. This can lead to heightened levels of anxiety, an overactive mind and feelings of scarcity or nervousness. We may lose our lust for life or experience a dullness in our interaction with the world. We may feel like we're in a 'fog', unable to prioritise or think clearly and decisively.

MENTAL & EMOTIONAL SYMPTOMS
The mental and emotional symptoms of a root chakra that is out of alignment stem from our lack of security and belonging.

- Low self-esteem
- Pessimism or limited thinking
- Heightened anxiety or nervousness
- Restlessness
- Lethargy and apathy
- Irritation and unwarranted anger
- Inability to focus
- Inflexibility

PHYSICAL SYMPTOMS
Physically, issues with our root chakra can manifest in the lower back, our legs and feet, the large intestine, the bladder and kidneys.

- Disordered eating, bingeing or loss of appetite
- Lower back pain
- Pain in the legs or feet
- Elimination issues, constipation or incontinence
- Weight gain or loss
- Lowered immunity

BENEFITS OF BALANCE

When the root chakra is aligned, we feel a wonderful sense of belonging. We know we are being cared for and are not fearful that our basic needs will not be met. We feel grounded in our body and connected to the earth, appreciative of its beauty and thankful for all it provides. Because our roots are healthy, we can easily weather change, moving through conflict with an even-keeled confidence. With a balanced root chakra, we are able to meet challenges with a grounded flexibility.

A State of Flow: When we tend to our root chakra we eat better. We sleep better. We feel supportive of and supported by our family and community. A balanced, open root chakra creates a lust for life, reigniting passion where perhaps our engagement had dulled. It heightens our feelings of love and connection. We are able to realise our self-worth and move through life with a secure steadfastness. Because of the root chakra's earth element, its energy makes us feel at home in nature, deeply connected to the earth and all its beings. It provides a peaceful knowing that we are where we should be and that all we need will be provided.

MULADHARA IN HARMONY

A balanced root chakra brings all the energetic riches of a thriving root system, one that is healthy and nourished.

- Stability
- Security
- Groundedness
- Confidence
- Passion
- Connection
- Clarity
- Calm
- Self-esteem

ROOT CHAKRA AFFIRMATION: 'I AM'

Each chakra is associated with a particular affirmation that encompasses what the energy centre represents. For the root chakra, it is 'I am'. It represents the physicality of *muladhara*: I am here, I am alive, I am safe, I am. For more root chakra affirmations, see page 36.

CRYSTALS

The crystals associated with *muladhara* offer deep grounding and vibrate with earth energy. Stones that have this steadying, rooting quality tend to be dark or red in colour. Though the following stones are all associated with the root chakra, each addresses a different area of healing with subtle energetic differences.

ARAGONITE

If you are feeling an overwhelming sense of restlessness, the reddish-orange and browns of aragonite can help alleviate it. This powerful but gently grounding stone has high earth energy, helping to physically connect you to the beauty and wonder of nature, while mentally and emotionally bringing you down to earth. Use it to help clear a mental fog.

Make some magic: Hold a piece of aragonite in your left hand while you engage in a root chakra–stimulating visualisation, like the one on page 36.

BLACK TOURMALINE

This inky stone is powerfully protective, repelling and dispelling negative energy to create a more positive space internally and externally. It can help clear root chakra blockages, boosting your connection to the earth with its centring pull. It is wonderful for bringing balance, laying the foundation for the alignment of all the chakras.

Make some magic: Keep a piece of black tourmaline on your desk (or wherever you spend the most time), to create a safe and stable space.

HAEMATITE

This silvery, black stone is the ultimate stabiliser. It has a centring effect, grounding us in our body and connecting our feet to the earth. It can be particularly good for working with an underactive root chakra, as it can help to calm irrational anxiety and excessive worry. It offers a feeling of safety and security, which boosts a balanced root chakra.

Make some magic: For a clearing, balancing and opening effect, lie down and place a piece of haematite over your root chakra – at the base of your spine if you are lying face down, or just above your pubic bone if you are on your back. Stay in position for several minutes.

SMOKY QUARTZ

This quartz stone featuring grey 'smoky' hues is wonderful to work with if your root chakra imbalance manifests as negative or pessimistic thinking. Its centring energy will help ground you while also providing a calming yet energising boost. If you find you are resistant to or fearful of change, smoky quartz can help clear that block.

Make some magic: Keep a piece of smoky quartz on your nightstand to bring positivity to your waking hours.

Opposite, clockwise from top: black tourmaline; smoky quartz; haematite; aragonite

ESSENTIAL OILS

Because the root chakra is associated with our sense of smell, working with essential oils to support *muladhara* can be especially beneficial. Here are a few earthy, grounding oils that are great for clearing and boosting root chakra energy, along with suggestions for use.

OIL	USE
Allspice* Allspice is a powerhouse for supporting the root chakra, because it can address both the mental/emotional and physical symptoms of imbalance. The warm, spicy oil, distilled from the small berries of the *Pimenta dioica* tree, has an aphrodisiac quality and can help calm anxiety and centre an overactive mind. It is also useful for assuaging digestive issues and easing muscle or joint pain.	For a grounding, cleansing experience, use allspice in the shower. Apply 3 drops to a wet flannel and brush it over your body, paying special attention to the root chakra location at your lower back. Breathe deeply throughout. 
Black Pepper** Another spicy scent, this warm oil is distilled from the small fruits of the flowering vine *Piper nigrum*. If you are dealing with a lack of focus or inability to concentrate, black pepper can help boost your mental acuity. It can also help ease anxiety. If you are feeling fatigued, black pepper can provide a bit of an energetic uplift. Physiologically speaking, it can help with indigestion and improve circulation.	To help alleviate brain fog, or for an instant boost of energy, dab a drop of black pepper oil on each temple and breathe deeply. 

OIL	USE
Cedarwood The rich, earthy scent of cedarwood, which comes from the wood chips and shavings of the *Cedrus atlantica* tree, provides an immediately grounding experience. Perfect for quelling overactive emotions, and offering a deep sense of comfort and security.	If you are feeling anxious or emotionally out of control, rub a drop of cedarwood between your palms, place your hands over your nose and deeply inhale.
Sandalwood Australian sandalwood offers earthy support in a bottle. Its rich and woody scent comes from the inner heartwood of *Santalum spicatum*, a small flowering tree. Less aromatically intense than the well-known Indian sandalwood, it has similar benefits – like grounding emotions and easing anxiety – and is much more sustainable.	Diffuse sandalwood in your bedroom to create a relaxing, peaceful environment. 
Vetiver Made from an actual root, that of the grass *Vetiveria zizanioides*, vetiver offers great root chakra support. Its strong woody scent is wonderfully grounding. It helps to ease restlessness and boost concentration. It can also help soothe the muscle or joint pain a *muladhara* imbalance can cause.	Add vetiver to a carrier oil and use it to treat joint or muscle pain by massaging the mixture into the affected area (see page 26).

*Do not use internally
**Do not use if pregnant or breastfeeding

ROOT CHAKRA MASSAGE OIL

A deeply grounding and uplifting blend with a hint of romantic floral.

INGREDIENTS

50 ml (1¾ fl oz) sweet almond oil
6 drops vetiver essential oil
4 drops sandalwood essential oil

2 drops bergamot essential oil
2 drops jasmine essential oil

Place ingredients in a bowl and stir to combine. Use a funnel to pour mixture into a dark blue or amber bottle. To use, rub a small amount between your palms and massage into skin. Repeat as needed.

FOOD

Because the root chakra is so intricately tied to feeling at home in our body, and connected to our physical being and environment, eating foods that support *muladhara* can be especially supportive when you are feeling symptoms of root chakra imbalance.

HEARTY, PROTEIN-RICH FOODS

Hearty, protein-rich foods like grains, nuts and legumes support the earthy groundedness of the root chakra, as do root vegetables of all kinds.

Grains: Opt for grains with a higher protein content like quinoa. Freekeh, an ancient grain that is becoming more commonplace, is another good option. Use either as the base in grain bowls or as an alternative ingredient for porridge.

Legumes: To have the grounding quality of legumes on hand, stock a variety of lentils – red, green, yellow or brown – for use in soups, salads or other main meals. They are packed with protein, fibre and nutrients, including iron, calcium and magnesium. Chickpeas are another type of high-protein legume. Add them to soups or salads, or turn them into hummus. They are packed with nutrients, including folate and manganese.

Nuts: Nuts and nut butters are another hearty, protein-rich food that supports the root chakra. Opt for almonds and cashews, which have a higher protein content than most nuts. Eat them plain as a healthy snack, scatter them on top of green salads for texture and added flavour or add nut butter to your morning smoothie or porridge.

Root vegetables: These are an easy, healthy go-to. Vegetables such as carrots, turnips, beetroot (beets), parsnips, sweet potatoes and swede (rutabaga) are packed with antioxidants, fibre, vitamins and minerals. And don't forget onions, which are high in vitamins B and C, as well as potassium.

RED FOODS

Because the root chakra is associated with red, on a vibrational level crimson-coloured foods can help support and heal *muladhara*. Plus red foods are rich in lycopene and ellagic acid, which can help to boost skin health.

Red apples: Be sure to eat the skin, which nearly doubles an apple's fibre and increases the amount of vitamins A, C and K. They can also help with elimination issues, a common symptom of root chakra imbalance.

 Berries: High in fibre, vitamin C and antioxidants, opt for red berries like strawberries and raspberries. Cranberries are also high in antioxidants (and great for urinary tract health), while goji berries are vitamin A powerhouses.

 Cherries: These small stone fruits are packed with fibre, vitamin C and potassium and are rich in antioxidants. Eat them by the handful as a delicious snack.

 Tomatoes: These are a great source of lycopene, an antioxidant that has been shown to reduce risk of heart disease and cancer. They are also packed with vitamins C and K, potassium and folate.

 Pomegranates: These seeds are like tiny, magenta jewels, and making them a part of your diet will add a wealth of vitamins C and K.

HERBS & SPICES

The spices that help balance the root chakra have an earthiness, or are actually roots themselves.

 Garlic: This has been used for culinary and medicinal purposes for centuries. It is a natural antibiotic.

 Paprika: Sprinkle this mild, earthy spice over roasted vegetables for added flavour.

 Cayenne: A dash of cayenne is an easy way to bring heat to a dish.

 Turmeric: This bitter root has powerful anti-inflammatory benefits. Use it to make tea or add to savoury dishes.

 Horseradish: This root is rich in antioxidants and adds an intense kick to sauces.

BEETROOT & APPLE JUICE

The gorgeous colour of your juice – a tasty way to drink your vegetables – resonates with the root chakra.

INGREDIENTS
3 red apples
1 beetroot (beet)
1 carrot

1 cm (½ in) piece of fresh turmeric, peeled

Cut all ingredients to fit into a juicer. Press through the juicer and stir before serving.

ROASTED ROOT VEGETABLE SALAD

This hearty salad will keep you grounded and nourished.

INGREDIENTS

3 baby carrots, halved

2 small beetroot (beets), boiled, peeled and cut into wedges

1 roma (plum) tomato, cut into wedges

¼ small sweet potato, cut into batons

2 tablespoons olive oil

2 garlic cloves. diced

salt and pepper

1 tablespoon hazelnuts

20 g (¾ oz) beetroot (beet) leaf or baby spinach leaves, roughly chopped

20 ml (¾ fl oz) balsamic vinegar

Preheat the oven to 180°C (350°F). Place the carrots, beetroot, tomato and sweet potato in a large bowl. In a small bowl, combine half of the olive oil, the diced garlic and season with salt and pepper. Stir, then pour over the vegetables and toss to coat. Spread the vegetables over a baking tray in a single layer. Roast for 15–20 minutes until all the vegetables are soft and starting to caramelise. Remove from the oven and cool slightly. Meanwhile, roast the hazelnuts for 5 minutes, then roughly chop and set aside. Combine the vegetables with the chopped leaves. Drizzle the remaining olive oil and vinegar over the vegetables and sprinkle with the roasted nuts to serve.

YOGA POSES

Each of these *asanas* has a rooting, grounding effect, connecting your being to the earth below it and helping to centre your body and mind. Try these poses when you are feeling out of balance..

TADASANA (Mountain Pose)
Stand tall with your feet firmly planted on the ground – feet hip-width apart as necessary. Gently rock back and forth and side to side then come to a standstill with your weight evenly distributed on the soles of your feet. Pull your shoulder blades back and down, opening your collarbones. Hang your arms next to your body, palms facing forward. Relax your jaw, soften your eyes and stay here for 30 seconds or more.

UTTANASANA (Standing Forward Fold)
From Mountain Pose, raise your arms up on the inhale then exhale and sweep your arms out and down, swan-diving with a flat back as you bend at the hips. Place your fingertips on the floor in line with your toes. With a slight bend in the knees, engage your quads and let your head hang. Stay for five full breaths. To come up, place your hands on your hips and slowly rise, keeping a flat back.

MALASANA (Garland Pose)
From Mountain Pose, move your feet wider than hip-width, almost to the edge of your mat, toes pointing slightly out. Bend your knees to come into a squatting position, sinking your hips low. Lean slightly forward between your thighs keeping your heels on the ground. Bring your palms together at your heart centre, hugging your inner thighs in while you push your knees out with your elbows. Drop your tailbone and lift the crown of your head. Stay here for 5–10 breaths. To come up, place your palms on the floor and push up into Standing Forward Fold.

BALASANA (Child's Pose)

Kneel, with the tops of your feet flat on your mat, big toes touching. Sit on your heels and widen your knees hip-width. Inhale to lengthen up, then exhale, folding your torso over and between your thighs. Lengthen your tailbone and root your forehead to the floor. Stretch your arms out in front, palms facing down on the mat. Rest here for a full minute, or as long as you like.

Mula Bandha

Known as the 'root lock', the practice of *mula bandha* is another way to support your root chakra. Simply put, *mula bandha* consists of contracting the muscles of the pelvic floor (not unlike the Kegel exercises that many women use to strengthen bladder control). On an energetic level, *mula bandha* is akin to a dam, stopping the flow of energy out of the body through the pelvis and instead redirecting it up through the other energy centres towards the crown of the head. Practise *mula bandha* in Garland Pose to help capture the energy of the pose.

VISUALISATION, MEDITATION & AFFIRMATIONS

ROOT YOURSELF

This standing meditation has a physical and energetically grounding effect (practising barefoot will increase its resonance). To begin, stand in Mountain Pose (page 34), with the weight of your feet evenly distributed. Rather than hang your arms to your sides, hold your left hand in your right hand and place them over your pelvic area. Close your eyes. With each exhalation allow your feet to feel heavier, more firmly grounded. Picture the energy of each exhalation flowing out from the soles of your feet into the ground like the roots of a big, beautiful tree. With each breath your roots grow stronger and deeper into the earth. Send your energy to their very tips. With your inhalation, use your roots to draw earth energy up and into your body. Let it fill your feet, then your legs, your pelvic area and flow on up the body. Repeat this visualisation, deepening your roots and drawing earth energy up, for five minutes. Open your eyes and feel the effects of this centring practice.

Sound Meditation

Each chakra has an associated sound, a 'seed syllable' known as the *bija* mantras. For *muladhara*, the sound is 'lam' (pronounced 'lahhhm'). Verbalising this sound and feeling its vibration in your body can help you connect to the root chakra's energy.

AFFIRMATIONS

Affirmations can be a powerful tool for working with any chakra. Use one of these suggestions, or let them inspire you to create your own personalised affirmation depending on the energy you need. Say it out loud to your reflection in the mirror in the morning and at night, or at the end of a yoga practice. You can also say it silently, whenever you want or need to.

I am strong and centred.
I am here and I am safe.
I am at home in my body.
I have all that I need to survive and thrive.
I am loved. I am supported. I belong.
I am focused and I choose calm.
I am rooted to the earth and connected
*   to the universe.*
My foundation is strong and my being
*   is flexible.*
I know myself. I love myself. I honour myself.

RITUALS & ACTIVITIES

Tapping into your root chakra energy can be a fun and playful experience as well. There are many ways to resonate with *muladhara*, some of which you probably already do. Bringing mindfulness to everyday activities can result in a more meaningful engagement and deeper purpose.

Get out in nature. One way to boost your connection to the earth is by getting out of the house and appreciating its beauty. Take a walk, watch the sunset at the beach, visit a park or plan a camping trip. This can even be as simple as taking some time to garden, connecting with the earth and the types of life it supports.

Drink dandelion root tea. The root chakra is about being present and grounded in the here and now. Incorporating a tea ritual with *muladhara*-supporting herbs is a wonderful way to practise this kind of mindfulness. First, clear your table, or the space where you want to sit to enjoy your tea. Then boil your water. Listen as the bubbles begin to rise and intensify. Pour water into your favourite mug and add your dandelion root–filled tea diffuser. Leave to steep until you are happy with the flavour. Sit quietly, watching the steam rise, feeling the heat of the mug in your hands, and taking deep breaths of the earthy scent. Savour each sip.

Give yourself a foot massage. Our feet ground us to the earth, so taking care of them can be a deeply centring practice. After a bath or shower, use the root chakra massage oil (see page 26) to rub each foot, using slow, deep motions. Choose one of the root chakra affirmations to repeat as you do so. When you are finished, rinse the oil off, or put socks on and let it soak into your skin.

Walk barefoot. When you don't have time to get out into nature, simply connecting your bare feet to the earth can be a quick, grounding fix. Also known as 'earthing', this practice has been shown to promote better sleep, help reduce pain and boost an overall sense of well-being.

Take a dance break. This could also be 'get physical' or 'exercise' but dancing gets the same results in an uplifting way. Plus it can be done when you need a break from your computer or while making dinner. Play one of your favourite songs and start moving your body in whatever way feels best.

SACRAL CHAKRA

Emotions + Sexuality + Creativity

Overview: The sacral chakra is the second chakra in our energetic system. It is located just below the navel and above the pelvic floor, right around the lower lumbar spine and the sacrum. If the root chakra helps lay the foundation for our physical connection to the earth and our bodies, the sacral chakra is the basis of our emotional well-being. It also governs our sexuality and creativity.

Sanskrit Name

Svadhisthana: In Sanskrit *swa* means 'one's own', while *adhisthana* means 'place' or 'dwelling'.

The sacral chakra can be thought of as our pleasure centre. It is where our passion lies, in all of its manifestations. The sacral chakra also corresponds to our reproductive organs and governs our sexuality. On a literal level, it represents fertility and procreation. But on a figurative level, this fertility can be thought of in terms of a full and fertile existence – all of the things in life that light us up. And ideologically speaking, 'creation' expands far beyond the physical generation of offspring. *Svadhisthana* governs all facets of our creativity – writing, cooking, making art, anything that stokes our passion for learning, doing and discovering. It is represented by the element of water, and a healthy sacral chakra puts us in the flow of energy and life, as though we are moving effortlessly along with a gentle current. It represents flexibility and freedom. A balanced sacral chakra permeates into many areas of our lives, creating healthy relationships, nurturing inspiration and creativity, helping us to seek and enjoy pleasure, physically, sensually, sexually. It provides a strong emotional foundation that allows us to not only live in the moment but to also truly enjoy it.

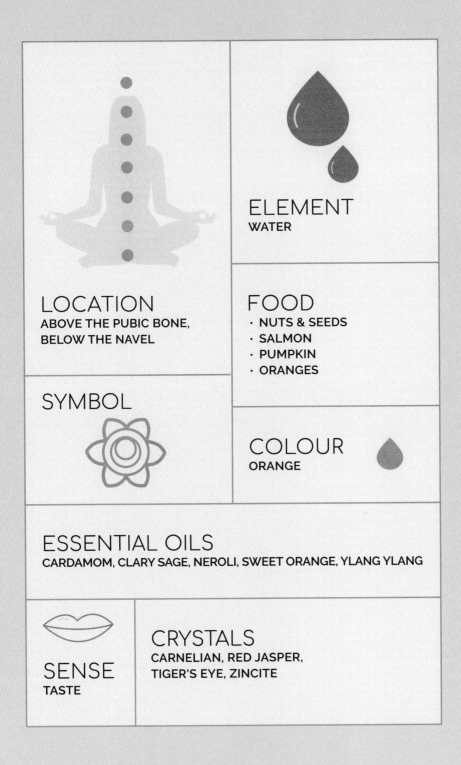

ELEMENT
WATER

LOCATION
ABOVE THE PUBIC BONE,
BELOW THE NAVEL

FOOD
- NUTS & SEEDS
- SALMON
- PUMPKIN
- ORANGES

SYMBOL

COLOUR
ORANGE

ESSENTIAL OILS
CARDAMOM, CLARY SAGE, NEROLI, SWEET ORANGE, YLANG YLANG

SENSE
TASTE

CRYSTALS
CARNELIAN, RED JASPER,
TIGER'S EYE, ZINCITE

SYMPTOMS OF IMBALANCE

An imbalanced sacral chakra can manifest in a number of different ways, not only mentally and emotionally, but in the body as well. If our *svadhisthana* needs tending to, we may see those consequences play out in our relationships, our sex life and also our creativity.

Overactive Chakra: An overactive sacral chakra can cause high drama in our relationships, whether romantic, sexual or platonic: mood swings, codependency, jealousy and more – all the fiery emotions and an inability to temper them. Sex may also be a problem. We could want too much of it at the expense of other forms of connection. Our physical needs may feel distracting and insatiable.

Underactive Chakra: When our sacral chakra is underactive those kinds of symptoms may swing the other way. We may feel little to no sex drive. We could feel as though the pleasure has been leached out of life, with clouds of apathy and depression. Our creativity could feel stunted, blocked or just plain non-existent. We might have trouble expressing ourselves creatively, authentically or sexually, or feel guilty when we do. Physically speaking we may experience fertility issues or sexual dysfunction.

MENTAL & EMOTIONAL SYMPTOMS

The mental and emotional symptoms of an unbalanced sacral chakra are tied to its main areas of focus: emotions, creativity and sexuality.

- Emotional instability
- Stifled creativity
- Feeling uninspired or disconnected from pleasure
- Lowered libido
- Guilt and shame
- Codependency
- Lack of feeling

PHYSICAL SYMPTOMS

Physically, issues with our sacral chakra can manifest in the lower back or pelvis, the large intestine, the bladder and the kidneys.

- Sexual dysfunction
- Reproductive or menstrual issues
- Fatigue
- Lower back pain or sciatica
- Urinary issues
- Kidney problems

BENEFITS OF BALANCE

When the sacral chakra is aligned we feel life and all of its pleasure open up to us. We experience a great sense of abundance, as though our cup overfloweth. We find enjoyment in our day-to-day existence, and greet the world with a sense of curiosity and playfulness. We know the things that light us up and feel free to pursue them with gusto, and we then feel deeply nourished by the pleasure they provide. We are inspired to create, whatever that may mean, and feel safe to do so.

A State of Flow: Tending to our sacral chakra in turn tends to our relationships. We may feel a stronger, healthier connection to our friends and partners. We are secure in the way we interact with and care for those closest to us and no longer fearful of emotional intimacy. We may feel more sensual, leaning in to the pleasures of our physical being, totally free and without an ounce of shame. Our sexual relationships become healthier too, unburdened by a sense of guilt or obligation. Because we are so secure in our feelings, there is a greater sense of balance – we have stepped off the exhausting emotional roller coaster of dramatic highs and lows. A steadfast passion runs through our very existence, igniting every experience with a greater sense of presence and joy.

SVADHISTHANA IN HARMONY

Balancing the sacral chakra builds on the stability of a balanced root chakra. Being grounded creates a springboard for living life to the fullest, and all that it entails.

- Adaptability
- Feelings of abundance
- Joy
- Creativity
- Passion
- Intimacy
- Pleasure
- Curiosity
- Fun and playfulness

SACRAL CHAKRA AFFIRMATION: 'I FEEL'

The affirmation associated with the sacral chakra is 'I feel', which taps directly into the pleasure and passion of this energy centre. It is where our emotions find their foundation and how we dig into the juiciness of life. For more sacral chakra affirmations, see page 56.

CRYSTALS

The crystals associated with *svadhisthana* can offer wonderful sparks of energy, helping to open the flow of creativity or passion. Stones that have this power to ignite are often the colour of flames. Although the following stones are associated with this chakra, each addresses a different area of healing with subtle energetic differences.

CARNELIAN

Carnelian is the crystal of passion. This fiery red stone has a mesmerising vibrancy, and is a powerful motivator. It is especially good for energising your creativity, which makes it a wonderful stone to work with if you are feeling stuck with an idea or uninspired by your work. Its energy brings a much-needed confidence.

Make some magic: For a clearing, balancing and opening effect, lie down and place a polished carnelian over your sacral chakra – at the top of the sacrum if you are lying face down, or just below your navel if you are on your back. Stay here in meditation for a few minutes.

RED JASPER

The deep grounding qualities of red jasper are well suited for tending to *svadhisthana*. Working with red jasper can spark energy and creativity and remind you of the joy in life. It can also awaken your sensuality, boost your libido or help forge a healthier sexual relationship with a partner.

Make some magic: To amplify the effect of a sacral chakra bath (page 46), add red jasper to the water before you get in.

TIGER'S EYE

The powerful balancing properties of this stone are great for bringing the sacral chakra into alignment, whether it is overactive or underactive. Much like the stones used for the root chakra, it has a grounding quality, but is especially good for *svadhisthana* as it works particular magic on the emotions.

Make some magic: If your emotions are feeling out of control, meditate with a piece of tiger's eye nearby.

ZINCITE

This red-orange crystal is like a little piece of pure passion. If life feels dull and uninspired, working with zincite can help give your energy a jump-start, reigniting your interest in all aspects of life – your work, your art, your relationships, yourself. Zincite is also a powerful manifestor, clearing energy so you can attune to your authentic self and call in the abundance you seek.

Make some magic: Hold a piece of zincite when saying your affirmations to boost your powers of manifestation, or place a piece over your sacral chakra as you do the visualisation on page 56.

Opposite, clockwise from top: carnelian; zincite; red jasper; tiger's eye

ESSENTIAL OILS

Because the sense of smell is so deeply connected to our sense of pleasure and sensuality too, essential oils can be incredibly effective when working with the sacral chakra. These range from spicy and earthy to floral and citrusy – all supporting a different aspect of *svadhisthana*.

OIL	USE
Cardamom This warm, gently spicy oil can help kickstart the energy of an underactive sacral chakra. Distilled from the dried fruit and seeds of *Elettaria cardamomum*, cardamom oil helps soothe while it energises. It is also a very sensual oil and can be used to stimulate feelings of intimacy and pleasure.	Add cardamom to a carrier oil and use it for a sacral chakra–stimulating massage, paying special attention to the lower lumbar and sacrum areas.
Clary Sage* The earthy scent of this grounding oil can help bring you into your body and feel the pleasure of the present moment. Distilled from the leaves and flowering tops of *Salvia sclarea*, clary sage has aphrodisiac properties too. It is also helpful for women whose sacral chakra imbalance is exacerbated by premenstrual syndrome (PMS) or the menopause.	To alleviate the discomfort of menstrual cramps, create a hot compress by mixing 10 drops clary sage oil in 250 ml (1 cup) hot water. Place a clean, folded flannel on top of the water, letting it soak up as much oil and water as possible. Wring out and place the compress over your abdomen.

OItL	USE

Neroli

The intoxicating scent of neroli is richly soothing and sensual. Distilled from the flowers of the bitter orange tree *Citrus aurantium*, this luxurious oil is wonderfully calming for an overactive sacral chakra. It is also an incredible mood booster, balancing and lifting unstable emotions.

For a sustained sense of well-being and a touch of sensuality, wear neroli as a fragrance by placing 1 drop of oil on the inside of each wrist.

Sweet Orange**

Sweet orange oil is like sunshine in a bottle. This energising, mood-boosting oil does wonders for our emotions. Cold pressed or distilled from the rinds of oranges from *Citrus sinensis*, this oil also resonates colourwise with the sacral chakra. With an uplifting scent that evokes joyfulness, this can be a nourishing oil for maintaining a balanced *svadhisthana*.

For a quick hit of happiness, rub a drop of orange oil between your palms, place your hands over your nose and inhale deeply.

Ylang Ylang

This incredibly fragrant oil distilled from the tropical flowers of *Cananga odorata* offers a direct line to pleasure through the olfactory system. Perfect for calming an overactive sacral chakra, it also has a very sensual scent, which can stoke feelings of intimacy and arousal. If you are feeling dull or uninspired, a deep inhale of ylang ylang can remind you of life's beauty.

Add ylang ylang to a carrier oil and add to warm water for a luscious, fragrant bath (see page 46).

*Do not use if pregnant or breastfeeding
**Do not use on skin that may be exposed to the sun

NOURISHING BATH OIL

Floral and citrusy, this sensual, calming, happy oil is a wonderful way to support the sacral chakra.

INGREDIENTS

3 tablespoons sweet almond oil
1 tablespoon jojoba oil
12 drops ylang ylang essential oil

12 drops sweet orange essential oil

Put all the ingredients into a small amber or dark blue jar or bottle and gently swirl to combine. To use, add 1–2 tablespoons to warm running bath water.

FOOD

Nourishing the sacral chakra with food and drink can help energise our body and balance our emotions. Taste can also offer a direct line to *svadhisthana*, the pleasure centre, especially if we take the time to be mindful and truly enjoy the food that nourishes us.

GOOD FATS & OMEGA-3S

Much like the sacral chakra helps regulate our emotions, foods rich in omega-3 fatty acids help regulate our energy and blood sugar levels, keeping us balanced.

Seeds: Flaxseeds (linseeds) and sesame seeds are easy ways to add sacral chakra support to a number of dishes. They are high in omega-3s, healthy fats that help fight inflammation and protect against chronic disease. Add them to smoothies or sprinkle them on top of soup.

Nuts: Nuts are another plant-based option for including omega-3s in your diet. These fatty acids also reduce the risk of heart disease and can help with the emotional symptoms of a *svadhisthana* imbalance by helping to alleviate anxiety and depression. Opt for nuts with the highest good-fat content, like almonds and walnuts.

Salmon: If you eat fish, then salmon can be a good way to bring *svadhisthana* into balance. It is packed with protein and omega-3 fatty acids. Cover it with almonds or pair with carrots for an effective *svadhisthana*-supporting meal.

ORANGE FOODS

Because the sacral chakra is associated with orange, enjoying foods in this colour can help stimulate *svadhisthana*. Orange foods are rich in vitamin C, which helps boost immunity. Beta-carotene and flavonoids can also be found in a number of orange foods, helping to lower blood pressure and LDL cholesterol (the bad kind). For a quick boost to *svadhisthana*, opt for juicy, water-dense fruits. For an overactive sacral chakra, try starchy vegetables to help balance the energy.

Pumpkin & squash: These squashes are packed with vitamins, minerals and antioxidants, and are high in fibre. They add a warmth to dishes and are perfect for roasting or blending into soups.

Carrots: Containing beta-carotene, which is good for eye health, carrots are high in potassium, vitamin K1 and antioxidants. Snack on them for a pick-me-up, or roast them as a *svadhisthana*-supporting side.

Oranges: In addition to being juicy and fragrant, oranges are a major source of vitamin C – one large orange contains the daily recommended amount. They are also high in fibre and flavonoids that can protect against heart disease.

Stone fruits: Orange stone fruits like peaches, apricots, nectarines and mangoes offer lots of juicy flavour and a wide variety of nutrients and minerals. Perfect for eating as a stand-alone snack or topping porridge or yoghurt in the morning.

Sweet potatoes: Sweet potatoes are another sweet and starchy food that can give your sacral chakra some sustained nourishment. Full of vitamins, minerals and fibre, they can also help fight inflammation. Opt for the garnet or jewel variety for their vibrant orange colour.

HERBS & SPICES

The spices that help balance the sacral chakra have a subtle spicy and energising warmth.

Cinnamon: The warm sweet flavour of this gentle spice is packed with antioxidants. Add to soups or porridge for extra flavour.

Cardamom: This sweet earthy spice can be very beneficial to digestion. If you are a coffee drinker, sprinkle it in your morning cup to make it easier on your stomach.

STAY HYDRATED

Since the sacral chakra is associated with water, staying hydrated is an important part of bringing it into alignment. Be sure to drink lots of fresh, filtered water (add a squeeze of orange for an extra boost). Coconut water can be especially hydrating and herbal teas like camomile pull double-duty, soothing the mind while nourishing the body.

MANGO PEACH SMOOTHIE

A sweet, hydrating drink that speaks to the sacral chakra.

INGREDIENTS

1 peach halved, stoned
    and sliced
70 g (2½ oz) frozen mango pieces

150 ml (5 fl oz) coconut water

Combine all the ingredients in a blender and blend until smooth.
Serve immediately.

BUTTERNUT PUMPKIN SOUP

This vibrant orange soup is packed with sacral chakra–nourishing seeds and spices.

INGREDIENTS

1 tablespoon olive oil
¼ onion, diced
1 garlic clove, diced
¼ teaspoon ground cumin
¼ teaspoon ground cinnamon
150 g (5½ oz) sweet potato,
    chopped

250 g (9 oz) butternut pumpkin
    (squash), peeled, seeded and cut
    into cubes
250 ml (1 cup) vegetable stock
100 ml (3½ fl oz) coconut milk
salt and pepper
1 teaspoon flaxseed (linseed) meal
1 teaspoon roasted pumpkin seeds

Heat the olive oil in a saucepan over medium heat, add the onion and fry for 3–4 minutes before adding the garlic, cumin and cinnamon. Stir, then add the sweet potato and pumpkin and stir through to coat. Add the stock and coconut milk, then season with salt and pepper and bring to the boil. Cover with a lid, reduce the heat and simmer until the vegetables are soft, about 20 minutes. Remove from the heat and blend until smooth. Serve with the flaxseed and pumpkin seeds sprinkled on top.

YOGA POSES

Loosening up the hip and pelvic area can help move stagnant energy through your sacral chakra.

UTKATA KONASANA (Goddess Pose)

From Mountain Pose (page 34), step your feet about 90 cm (3 ft) then pivot on your heels so your feet are parallel. Turn your toes out so they point to the corners of your mat. On the exhale, bring your hips down to a squat so that your thighs are parallel to the ground, keeping your knees directly over your ankles. Extend your arms to the sides then bend your elbows so your palms face forward in cactus arms. Tuck your tailbone slightly, lift the crown of your head to the ceiling and hold for five breaths.

PRASARITA PADOTTANASANA (Wide-legged Forward Fold)

From Goddess Pose, straighten your legs and turn your feet parallel, placing your hands on your hips. Lifting the crown of your head, hinge at the hips keeping a flat back as you slowly fold over. Place your palms on the ground, shoulder-width apart. If you are able, fold deeper, bending your elbows and bringing the crown of your head to your mat. Engage *mula bandha* by lifting the pelvic floor. Stay here for five breaths. To come up, bring your hands to your hips, and slowly raise your torso keeping a flat back. Bring your feet together and return to Mountain Pose.

EKA PADA RAJAKAPOTASANA (Pigeon Pose)

From Downward-facing Dog (page 94), lift your right leg then bring your knee forward, placing it on your mat next to your right hand, bringing your shin as parallel to the top of your mat as possible. Flex your right foot and lower your hips so that they are even, making sure your left toes are stretched out straight behind you. Stay here for a few breaths then walk your arms forward, folding over your shin until your forehead rests on the mat. Once you are comfortable in this modified pose, you can raise your torso, bend your left knee and grab your left foot with your left hand, elbow pointing up. Reach your chest to the sky, drop your head back and grab your left foot with your right hand, elbow pointing up. Stay here for five breaths then come back to Downward-facing Dog and repeat on the other side.

USTRASANA (Camel Pose)

Start by kneeling with your knees hip-width apart. Root your shins into the floor and place your hands on your sacrum, fingers facing down. Lean back, lift your chest, chin slightly tucked; reach your tailbone down creating space in the lower back. Stay here or go deeper by engaging your core and dropping your hands to your heels, your fingers over the soles of your feet (if you feel any compression in your lower back, return to the modified pose). Keeping your chest lifted, drop your head back. To come up, tuck your chin, bring your hands to your sacrum, and engage your core to lift yourself up.

BADDHA KONASANA (Bound Angle Pose)

Come to a seated position on your mat and bring the soles of your feet together, drawing your heels towards your pelvis and allowing your knees to open towards the floor. Hold your feet and press the soles together. Ground your sitting bones and extend through the crown of your head. Stay here or fold over, bringing your forehead to your feet. Stay here for five breaths, then slowly come up.

VISUALISATION, MEDITATION & AFFIRMATIONS

RIDING THE WAVES

Lie down or sit in a comfortable position and close your eyes. Take three deep breaths, inhaling through your nose and exhaling through your mouth. Clap your hands together and quickly rub them back and forth, generating heat and energy between your palms. Place your hands over your sacral chakra underneath your navel. Visualise a small spinning orange sphere where *svadhisthana* is located. As the sphere gets clearer and more vibrant, notice that the orange colour begins rolling off it in waves, first in tiny ripples then in larger undulations. Continue breathing as you see the colour roll in and out, reaching further each time until the orange light has filled your whole body with joy. Acknowledge the pleasure you feel throughout your body and open your eyes.

Sound Meditation

The seed syllable, or *bija* mantra, for *svadhisthana* is 'vam' (pronounced 'vahhhm'). Focus on your sacral chakra as the vibration moves through you.

AFFIRMATIONS

Using affirmations with your sacral chakra in mind will help connect you to your pleasure centre, and stoke your passion and creativity. Use one of the following suggestions, or let them inspire you to create your own personalised affirmation depending on the energy you need. Say it out loud to your reflection in the mirror in the morning and at night, or at the end of a yoga practice. You can also say it silently, whenever you want or need to.

I am a joyful being.
I attract healthy connections with people who love and respect me.
I love my body and honour what brings it pleasure.
I am fully awake to the wonders of the world.
I cherish all this life has to offer.
I feel confident and secure in my sexuality and I am safe to explore it.
I am awash with abundance.
I honour my emotions and feel through them as they come.
I'm a creative being filled with passion and inspiration.
The universe provides and I'm in its flow.

RITUALS & ACTIVITIES

Activating your sacral chakra is about embracing life and all its pleasures. Look for the fun in what you are doing and feel free to get creative, which truly gets to the essence of *svadhisthana*.

Take a bath. Since *svadhisthana* is associated with water, enjoying a nice warm bath is a wonderful way to connect with its essence. Make it a truly pleasurable experience by dimming the lights, lighting candles and having a clean, fresh, luxurious towel ready. Evoke even more sacral energy by using an essential oil bath oil (page 46), or bring some crystal magic by soaking with water-safe stones that support the sacral chakra.

Try something new. Tapping into creativity will help jump-start the inspiring energy of the sacral chakra and the most effective way of doing this is by trying something new. Get creative in the kitchen, by cooking or baking a new dish or using unfamiliar ingredients. Or break out the art supplies and explore an unfamiliar medium. Try an exercise class you have never been to, start a project that piques your interest or invite a new friend for coffee.

Visit somewhere you have never been. Travel is one of the most eye-opening ways to reconnect with wonder, but you don't have to plan a major trip to stoke that passion. Often simply exploring a nearby city or even just a new-to-you neighbourhood can reignite your passion for the world.

Indulge your sensuality. You don't need a partner to engage in this activity. In fact, indulging your sensuality on your own might make it even easier to be completely present in your body and find authentic pleasure in its sensations. Notice the feeling of touch when your fingers connect to your skin. Focus on your breathing and the sensations that arise. If your mind starts to wander, bring it back to the physical feelings you are experiencing.

Take up journalling. Feeling more connected to your feelings and understanding how to process them in healthy ways can help clear and activate the energy of the sacral chakra. One way to do this is by processing your emotions through words. Try writing in a notebook every day for a week, noting how you feel, what moods or emotions change, what you might be ignoring and what is deeply moving through you.

SOLAR PLEXUS CHAKRA

Identity + Self-worth + Personal Power

Overview: The third chakra in our energetic system, the solar plexus chakra, is the last of the lower chakras. It is located in the upper abdomen, just above the navel, by the stomach, diaphragm and mid-back. The solar plexus chakra is our centre of identity. It governs our confidence and sense of worth. It is the foundation of who we are, and how we move in the world.

Sanskrit Name

Manipura: *Mani* means 'jewel' in Sanskrit, while *pura* means 'place' or 'city'. *Manipura* is often translated as lustrous gem.

The solar plexus chakra is our essence, our ego, our conscious self. It drives our authenticity and gives us purpose. It is related to self-esteem and personal power, drive and motivation. Physically it governs our digestive system, and many of the organs involved, including the stomach, liver and pancreas. It is represented by fire – it gives us the internal fire we need to move forward, to transform with life's changes, to achieve our dreams in a healthy and fulfilling way. But the solar plexus chakra also governs our digestive fire, running the system that helps fuel us, that makes us strong. A well-balanced *manipura* gives us a true sense of self, and helps us understand our life's purpose. When we feel confident in who we are and driven by authentic dreams, forward motion is a given, plans easily fall into place and when they don't, we have enough trust in ourselves and the universe to know they will when the time is right. Taking care of our solar plexus chakra is like tending to our very essence, laying the foundation for feeling good about who we are and where we are going.

LOCATION
UPPER ABDOMEN, AT THE DIAPHRAGM, MID-BACK

SYMBOL

ELEMENT
FIRE

FOOD
- **ONIONS & BELL PEPPERS**
- **BEANS**
- **BANANAS**
- **PINEAPPLE**

COLOUR
YELLOW

ESSENTIAL OILS
ANISE SEED, FENNEL, HELYCHRISUM, LEMON, PEPPERMINT

SENSE
SIGHT

CRYSTALS
CITRINE, GOLDEN TOPAZ, PYRITE, YELLOW CALCITE

SYMPTOMS OF IMBALANCE

When our solar plexus chakra is out of alignment, it can wreak havoc on how we feel about ourselves and can make our path to a purpose seem more challenging. Physically an imbalanced *manipura* can manifest as a number of digestive issues.

Overactive Chakra: When our solar plexus chakra is overactive, we may find our ego getting the best of us. We may feel a need to control and dominate or we may be derailed by an obsession with perfection. We could be quick to anger and have intense bouts of productivity without being able to maintain a sense of sustained motivation.

Underactive Chakra: When our solar plexus chakra is blocked or stagnant, our self-worth really takes a hit. We may feel powerless and insignificant. We may be out of touch with our authentic self, which can lead to difficulty with decision-making or an inability to express ourselves. We may feel as though we have no guiding light or that the obstacles to our dreams are too big to overcome.

MENTAL & EMOTIONAL SYMPTOMS

An imbalanced solar plexus chakra leads to a rocky sense of self, and the detrimental feelings that stem from it.

- Low self-esteem
- Obsessive perfectionism
- Lack of purpose
- Feelings of insecurity
- Inability to be our authentic self
- Trouble making decisions
- Feelings of victimhood
- Controlling or overly ambitious

PHYSICAL SYMPTOMS

Since the solar plexus chakra governs our gut, most physical manifestations of an imbalance result in digestive issues.

- Indigestion
- Acid reflux
- Elimination issues
- Nausea
- Bloating or belly pain
- Diabetes

BENEFITS OF BALANCE

When we move through the world with authentic self-assuredness and good-hearted confidence we can know that our solar plexus chakra is open and balanced. We have a clear path, we know we are doing exactly what feels right for us, and we have a sense of self that cannot be deterred by others or our environment. Because our self-worth isn't in question, we also raise others up, working towards a better world for all.

A State of Flow: Bringing *manipura* into harmony helps us tend to ourselves so that we can tend to others. It fills us with a sense of purpose and puts us in the flow of our dreams, making their achievement seem and feel inevitable. We are motivated by its quiet yet powerful strength and warmth. It stokes our inner warrior so that we are able to face all of life's twists and turns. Rather than get derailed by a challenge, we know to view it as a valuable teaching moment, pushing us towards greater growth and success. It strengthens our gut instinct, so we can tap into what we know is right. A balanced *manipura* is embodied empowerment, which makes us radiant with strength and ability.

MANIPURA IN HARMONY

Balancing our solar plexus chakra brings the work we have done on our root and sacral chakras to fruition. It is the manifestation of coming into our own – a true sense of self. A balanced solar plexus chakra brings greater:

- Confidence
- Motivation
- Sense of identity
- Purpose
- Manifestation
- Strength
- Self-worth
- Empowerment
- Resilience

> ### SOLAR PLEXUS CHAKRA AFFIRMATION: 'I CAN'
> The solar plexus chakra wakes us up to our potential, and clears the path for us to follow our dreams. It provides the confidence and the motivation. Its affirmation is 'I can'. For more solar plexus chakra affirmations, see page 76.

CRYSTALS

The crystals that resonate with the solar plexus chakra practically glow with warmth and positivity. They are confidence boosters and powerful manifestors that help bring balance to your sense of abundance. Although the following stones are all beneficial for working with *manipura*, each addresses a different area of healing.

CITRINE

Citrine hits all the notes of what bringing the solar plexus chakra into alignment means. It is a powerful stone of manifestation, but it will teach you that abundance has more to do with perspective than material goods. It also enhances self-confidence to help you navigate setbacks and achieve your authentic desires.

Make some magic: A small piece of tumbled citrine makes a perfect pocket stone, or a wonderful piece of jewellery.

GOLDEN TOPAZ

The warmth and gentle energy of this sun-kissed crystal will help energise your mind and flood you with inspiration. It is a stone of attraction, aligning you with your desires and drawing abundance to you. But it is also a poignant teacher, ensuring that success doesn't override the purity of your intentions.

Make some magic: If you have an underactive solar plexus chakra, bathe your golden topaz in sunlight to boost its masculine energy. Then have it nearby while you do *manipura*-opening yoga poses (page 74) to enhance the flow.

PYRITE

Pyrite is perfectly suited for supporting the solar plexus chakra. It has a grounding, empowering effect, and can help you focus while propelling you forward. Its masculine energy boosts confidence and clears a path for attraction and abundance.

Make some magic: Pyrite is a wonderful workplace stone. Keep a piece on your desk for its radiant force of protection, positivity and potential.

YELLOW CALCITE

If you have noticed a pattern of behaviour born of a solar plexus chakra imbalance, yellow calcite can help clear that old energy and make way for a new path of personal empowerment. Its sunny vibrations will help energise and motivate you. It opens the path for guidance from the divine, helping you to find the purpose you seek.

Make some magic: For a clearing, balancing and opening effect, lie down and place a piece of yellow calcite over your solar plexus chakra – mid-back if you are lying face down, or just above your navel if you are on your back. Stay here for several minutes.

Opposite, clockwise from top: yellow calcite; citrine; pyrite, golden topaz

ESSENTIAL OILS

Essential oils can help treat the mental and physical symptoms of solar plexus chakra imbalance. These bright and earthy oils are good for alleviating digestive issues and/or offering a zing of energy.

OIL	USE
Anise Seed* ** This versatile oil has a liquorice-like scent, and is used to address a wide range of gastro-intestinal issues. The seeds of the herb *Pimpinella anisum* are steam-distilled to create this earthy oil, which can alleviate nausea and help aid digestion.	If you are feeling nauseous, rub a drop of anise seed oil between your palms, cover your nose and inhale deeply. Repeat as needed.
Fennel* * ******* Fennel oil is a wonderful detoxifier that can also boost self-esteem, perfect for nourishing an underactive solar plexus chakra. Steamed from the seeds of the flowering herb *Foeniculum vulgare*, fennel oil is also helpful in treating digestive issues, especially bloating and gassiness.	For relief from bloating or indigestion, mix 6 drops fennel oil in 1 tablespoon carrier oil and massage directly onto the abdomen.

*Do not use internally
**Do not use on skin that may be exposed to the sun
***Do not use while pregnant or breastfeeding
****Do not use if you have epilepsy or are prone to seizures

OIL	USE

Helichrysum ***

This sweet, earthy oil comes from *Helichrysum italicum*, an herb topped with clusters of tiny yellow flowers that resonate with the solar plexus chakra. It is an incredibly healing oil – it can soothe irritated skin and reduce scarring – and energetically, it is thought to help us face challenges with persistence and authenticity.

If you are facing a big challenge and need a little energetic boost, mix a drop of helichrysum with a drop of carrier oil and dab the mixture on each temple. Close your eyes and take three deep breaths.

Lemon

This bright, citrusy oil can be just the zing your *manipura* needs. Much like sweet orange resonates with the sacral chakra, lemon, cold pressed from the rinds of the *Citrus limon* fruits, vibrates with the yellow energy of the solar plexus chakra. Use it for re-invigoration and overall mood boosting and motivation.

Diffuse lemon in the home for a bright and happy environment that feels ripe with new energy. See the blend on page 66 to boost the solar plexus chakra.

Peppermint ***

The energising aroma of peppermint can boost your mood, focus and drive. Steam-distilled from *Mentha* x *piperita*, this minty oil is an energy powerhouse, lifting the spirits and helping to clear the mind. It is also beneficial in alleviating the digestive issues that an imbalance or block in the solar plexus chakra can cause.

Peppermint can help boost clarity; try incorporating it into your meditation practice. Before you begin, rub 1 drop peppermint oil between your palms, cover your nose and inhale deeply.

SOLAR PLEXUS-BOOSTING DIFFUSION

Warm, earthy and brightly citrusy, this blend will motivate and inspire you.

INGREDIENTS

3 drops lemon essential oil
1 drop helichrysum essential oil
2 drops cedarwood essential oil

100 ml (3½ fl oz) water

The new moon is a time of fresh starts, new ideas and powerful manifestation – a great time to connect with your solar plexus chakra. Create an energising environment around the new moon by combining these ingredients in your home diffuser.

FOOD

Since the solar plexus chakra governs digestion, nourishing its energy with food and drink can be especially effective. There are a number of ways to do this: with foods that stoke our digestive fire, with complex carbohydrates that offer sustained energy, and yellow foods that vibrate on the same frequency as *manipura*.

PUNGENT, SOUR & SALTY FOODS
If you have an underactive solar plexus chakra, try incorporating pungent, sour and salty foods associated with boosting *agni* – our digestive fire.

Onions & bell peppers (capsicums): While the pungency of onions is beneficial for the solar plexus chakra, they are also rich with antioxidants. Chillies are another way to add pungency (and heat!) to your diet and they have a surprising amount of vitamins and minerals.

Fermented foods: Foods like kimchi and sauerkraut are extremely flavourful and full of probiotics. Add them to grain bowls for a fermented kick. Miso, a paste made from fermented soybeans, adds a umami taste to soups, sauces and marinades. Add kefir or yoghurt to your morning routine, for a dairy-based boost of beneficial cultures. Vinegar is another fermented kitchen staple; add it to dressings.

Beans: Kidney beans and black beans are two good sources of energy-providing foods, especially because they also contain protein, which makes the energy they impart longer lasting. Both are also good sources of iron, B vitamins and essential minerals like manganese and magnesium.

Grains: Whole grains can be a good source of energy as well as iron, minerals and B vitamins. If you opt for sprouted grains (or sprout your own), they offer even more nutrients. Try making a breakfast porridge from sprouted millet or baking with sprouted flour.

YELLOW FOODS
Since yellow is the colour associated with *manipura*, incorporating yellow foods can resonate with the energy of the solar plexus chakra. Like sacral-supporting orange foods, yellow foods are also rich in immunity-boosting vitamin C, beta-carotene and flavonoids. They are also good sources of fibre.

Bananas: These sweet fruits are high in fibre and a good source of potassium, which helps nerve and muscle function. Eat atop a bowl of sprouted whole grain porridge for a *manipura*-friendly meal.

Sweetcorn: This is also high in fibre and B vitamins, and is a good source of essential minerals including zinc and manganese. Pop for a light snack, or pickle for a flavourful relish that boosts its *manipura*-supporting colour with the *agni*-boosting power of fermentation.

Lemons: The bright yellow of lemons is matched by their uplifting scent and burst of tart, sweet, sour flavour. They are high in vitamin C. Because many of their benefits come from the pulp and the rind, try using the zest when making dishes. Preserved lemons are a delicious addition to grain bowls and dressings.

Pineapple: Another sweet, juicy fruit that is packed with vitamins, minerals and antioxidants. It also contains bromelain, an enzyme that can help aid digestion.

WHAT IS AGNI?

In the Ayurvedic tradition, the digestive system is at the heart of good health, and *agni* can be considered the 'digestive fire'. When our *agni* is healthy, our body efficiently turns food into nutrients, so that every system can run optimally. When our *agni* is low or imbalanced, it can cause a host of issues throughout the body. Help keep your *agni* healthy by drinking room-temperature water, having your largest meal at lunch, and eating mindfully (page 129).

HERBS & SPICES

The spices that help balance the solar plexus chakra have a little zing and, in the case of turmeric, incredibly vibrant colour.

Ginger: The warming effect of this spicy, fibrous root can be a great tonic – it is anti-inflammatory, good for circulation and boosts digestion. Add it to stir-fries, soups or use to make tea.

Turmeric: This bitter root is known for the bright yellow colour it imparts and its powerful anti-inflammatory benefits. Turmeric is great for curries and soups.

GINGER TURMERIC TEA

A warming, anti-inflammatory tea is perfect for nourishing the solar plexus chakra.

INGREDIENTS

1-2 cm (½-¾ in) piece of ginger, peeled and sliced

1-2 cm (½-¾ in) piece of fresh turmeric, peeled and sliced

250 ml (1 cup) water

3 slices of lemon, set 1 slice aside to serve

Preparation: 5 mins | **Cook time:** 10 mins | **Makes:** about 250 ml (1 cup)

Combine the ingredients in a saucepan. Bring to the boil, then cover with a lid, reduce the heat and simmer for 3–4 minutes. Strain and serve with fresh lemon.

PICKLED SWEETCORN RELISH

This tangy relish pairs 'digestive fire'–boosting ingredients with the solar plexus chakra's bright yellow colour.

INGREDIENTS

3 tablespoons white sugar
120 ml (4 fl oz) apple cider vinegar
½ teaspoon black mustard seeds
½ teaspoon paprika
salt and pepper
2 sweetcorn cobs

1 heirloom tomato, peeled and
    finely chopped
½ red bell pepper (capsicum), diced
1 small red onion, diced
2 tablespoons finely chopped
    coriander (cilantro) leaves

Place the sugar, vinegar, mustard seeds and paprika together in a small bowl, season with salt and pepper and mix until the sugar has dissolved. Remove the husks from the sweetcorn and cut off the kernels with a knife into a saucepan, saving any juice as you go. Add the remaining ingredients to the pan, then pour over the pickling liquid. Bring to the boil, then reduce the heat to low and simmer gently for about 20 minutes. Make sure to watch the liquid levels, if the heat is too high, it may burn easily. Cool and transfer the mixture to a sterilised jar. Keep refrigerated and use within 3–4 weeks.

YOGA POSES

Building strength, engaging the core and twisting through the torso can light up your solar plexus chakra.

PHALAKASANA (Plank)

From Downward-facing Dog (page 94), lower your hips keeping your legs straight and bring your torso towards the floor until it is parallel with the mat. Your arms should be straight, shoulders directly over your wrists. Root your hands to the floor, pull your belly in and pull your shoulders onto your back. Straighten your neck, looking down at the floor, and lengthen your tailbone, making a long, straight line from the crown of your head to your heels. Stay here for five breaths, then return to Downward-facing Dog.

VIRABHADRASANA I (Warrior I)

From Mountain Pose (page 34), step your feet wide apart. Turn to the right, turning your right foot out, so the toes face the short end of your mat, and turning your left foot in at a 45-degree angle. Square your hips to the short end of your mat, keeping your left foot planted, and bend your right knee over your right ankle. Inhale to reach up through your arms, lengthening through the spine, and bring your palms together over your head. Pull your shoulders down and gently tilt your head back. Stay here for five breaths. Return to Mountain Pose and repeat on the other side.

VIRABHADRASANA II (Warrior II)

From Mountain Pose, step or jump the feet wide apart, facing the long side of your mat. Turn your right foot so the toes face the front of your mat, allowing your left hip to swing slightly forward. Keeping your chest open, extend your arms in a straight line over your legs at shoulder-height, palms facing down. Bend your right knee over the right ankle, thigh parallel to the floor. Press your left foot into the floor. Draw your tailbone down and the crown of your head up, lengthening the spine. Turn your head to the right looking out over your fingers. Stay here for five breaths. Return to Mountain Pose and repeat on the other side.

PARIVRTTA TRIKONASANA (Revolved Triangle)

From Mountain Pose, step your left foot back then turn to face the side of your mat with your legs wide apart, feet parallel. Extend your arms in a straight line at shoulder-height, palms facing down. Turn your right foot so your toes face the front of your mat and turn your left foot in at a 45-degree angle. Turn your hips to face the short end of your mat, arms still out to the side. Rotate your pelvis, torso and head to the right so your left arm extends over your right leg. Hinge at the hip bringing your left fingers down to the outside of the right foot, raising your right arm perpendicular to the floor, fingers to the ceiling. Straighten your neck and look to the side. Inhale to lengthen the spine, exhale to twist a little deeper. Stay here for five breaths. Return to Mountain Pose and repeat on the other side.

PARIPURNA NAVASANA (Boat Pose)

Start from a seated position, knees bent, feet to the floor. Keeping your knees together, slowly raise your feet, toes pointed, until your shins are parallel with the mat. Lean your torso slightly back, keeping your spine straight. Lift your chest, pull your shoulders back and raise your arms parallel to the ground, palms facing up. Stay here, or straighten your legs to a 45-degree angle, palms facing each other. Balance on your sitting bones, engaging the core. Stay here for five breaths.

VISUALISATION, MEDITATION & AFFIRMATIONS

LIGHT YOUR FIRE

Sit in a comfortable seated position in a darkened room, in front of a stable surface. Light a candle and set it on the surface. With your eyes closed, take three deep, cleansing breaths, inhaling through your nose and exhaling through your mouth, releasing any tension with every exhalation. Open your eyes and softly gaze at the candle's flame, letting its quiet flicker fill your mind. Gently place your hands over your solar plexus chakra, just above your navel. Close your eyes and picture the candle's flame where your solar plexus chakra is. Imagine the flame slowly grows bigger, burning more brightly. Feel its warmth and energy radiate out from your solar plexus chakra, until every cell of your body is filled with its enveloping yellow light. Feel it fill you with a readiness to embrace your true self, and move forward with purpose. Acknowledge your power, open your eyes, thank the candle for its guiding light and blow out the flame.

Sound Meditation

The seed syllable, or *bija* mantra, for *manipura* is 'ram' (pronounced 'rahhhm'). Chant it slowly letting the sound and vibration wash over your solar plexus chakra.

AFFIRMATIONS

Balance the energy of your solar plexus chakra with affirmations that will help you step into your power. Use one of the following suggestions, or let them inspire you to create your own personalised affirmation depending on the energy you need. Say it out loud to your reflection in the mirror in the morning and at night, or at the end of a yoga practice. You can also say it silently, whenever you want or need to.

I am confident in my capabilities.
I am at peace with my true self.
I am strong.
I am worthy of all the universe has to offer.
I love myself unconditionally.
My intuition is powerful and I honour my instincts.
I am open to my life's purpose and excited to pursue it.
I am powerful and empowered.
I know who I am. I love who I am. I honour who I am. I am proud of who I am.
I have everything I need to achieve my dreams.

RITUALS & ACTIVITIES

Tapping into the solar plexus chakra is about finding your inner fire, being true to yourself, and clearing the way for your dreams to manifest. Do what feels authentic to your own *manipura* journey.

Enjoy a fire. To fan your inner flame, enjoy a fire, whether it is at home in a fireplace or an outdoor bonfire. Sit with the fire, watching the flames leap and the sparks pop, feeling its warmth on your body. If you'd like, write down any old patterns that no longer serve you or negative feelings you are ready to let go of on pieces of paper, and add the paper to the fire. Watch it burn and feel the release.

Soak up some sun. To balance the sun of your energetic system, it can help to soak up the warmth and light of the sun that rules our solar system. Take a walk on a sunny day, sit in a park and feel the rays on your skin, or simply perch by a light-facing window and enjoy the way the sun fills the room.

Clean up and buy flowers. One of the keys to making our dreams manifest is making room for them to unfold. Often we can do this by clearing space in the physical realm. Clean up your living space to jump-start *manipura* energy. Clear out old items you no longer use, and give your most used room a deep and thorough clean. Then treat yourself to some fresh-cut flowers in beautiful yellow hues, like sunflowers, ranunculus or tulips.

Listen to and honour your gut. Trusting our gut isn't always easy, especially if we have an underactive solar plexus chakra and have felt disconnected from our intuition. Practise tuning in to what your body is telling you by actively bringing awareness to your gut instincts. If you have a decision to make, sit quietly with your thoughts, see what comes up and honour what feels true. Start with something small to familiarise yourself with the feelings. The more awareness you foster, the easier it will be to tap into your truths.

Build strength. Feeling strong in our physical body can help us connect to our inner strength as well. If you are already an active person, try doing something that challenges your body in a new way, like rock climbing or roller-skating. If you are new to strength training, start small by incorporating light weightlifting, push-ups or sit-ups into your regular exercise habits.

HEART CHAKRA

Love + Compassion + Connection

Overview: The heart chakra is the fourth chakra in our energetic system; it is the bridge between the lower physical chakras, which relate to us and who we are on this planet, and the upper spiritual ones, which go beyond the physical realm. It is located exactly where you think it would be – the centre of the chest – and is beautifully, wonderfully all about love. How we love ourselves, others and the world around us.

> **Sanskrit Name**
> **Anahata:** *Anahata* translates to 'unstruck', and references the idea of the unstruck sound, the cosmic force always vibrating within us, that we can only truly hear when we are able to quieten the body and the mind. It is also loosely translated to 'unhurt', which is an incredibly powerful way to think about our heart chakra.

Anahata is our heart centre. It governs how we love. The love we give ourselves, the love we give others, the love we receive. It is the centre for love in all of its capacities – romantic, platonic, familial, divine and beyond. Love can spark incredible transformation – an emotional plane that extends beyond our physical existence. It is no mistake that our heart chakra is represented by air, the very element that becomes our life force when we take it in through our breath. Love is also something we cannot truly live without. Compassion, kindness, forgiveness and empathy are all lessons of *anahata*. And its reign goes further than the love we have for those in our lives. The heart chakra is the bridge between our material and spiritual worlds; between our physical consciousness and a higher one. It reveals the unity inherent in our very existence. We are all connected – one love – to one another, to the earth and to every living thing on it. The heart chakra teaches us to live in that truth.

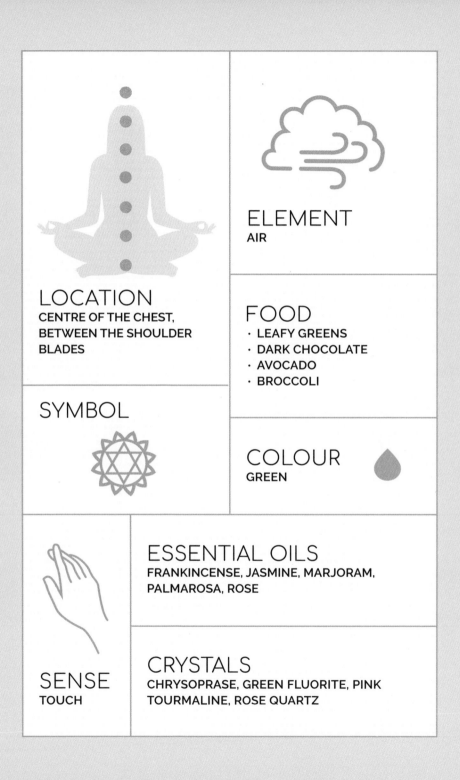

LOCATION

CENTRE OF THE CHEST, BETWEEN THE SHOULDER BLADES

SYMBOL

ELEMENT

AIR

FOOD
· LEAFY GREENS
· DARK CHOCOLATE
· AVOCADO
· BROCCOLI

COLOUR

GREEN

ESSENTIAL OILS
FRANKINCENSE, JASMINE, MARJORAM, PALMAROSA, ROSE

CRYSTALS
CHRYSOPRASE, GREEN FLUORITE, PINK TOURMALINE, ROSE QUARTZ

SENSE
TOUCH

SYMPTOMS OF IMBALANCE

Because as a culture we are so familiar with matters of the heart, it is easy to see and understand the symptoms that might arise from an *anahata* imbalance. All of the emotional effects have to do with our feelings of love and connection – an overzealousness or withdrawal. Neither is healthy nor sustainable. Physical manifestations lie mostly in the heart and respiratory areas.

Overactive Chakra: An overactive heart chakra can lead to a lack of healthy boundaries. We may give too much or exaggerate a sense of connection where there aren't really authentic feelings. We may experience extreme jealousy, insecurity or codependency.

Underactive Chakra: A blocked *anahata*, whether from past heartbreak or trauma, can lead to feelings of disconnection and withdrawal. We may steep in the grievances or 'failures' of our past relationships, which can keep us mired in the habit of looking back rather than connecting and loving and living in the present. We may feel unable to love ourselves, and resistant, suspicious or disbelieving when it comes to receiving love from someone else.

MENTAL & EMOTIONAL SYMPTOMS

An imbalanced heart chakra can lead to a whole host of issues around our ability to give and receive love.

- Jealousy or codependence
- Lack of compassion
- Disconnection with self and others
- Feeling undeserving of love
- Inability to forgive, grudge-holding
- Lack of trust and authentic connection
- Loneliness and depression
- Judgemental thoughts and self-criticism

PHYSICAL SYMPTOMS

Anahata governs the heart, our circulatory system, the chest, lungs and upper back.

- Blood pressure problems
- Poor circulation
- Heart problems
- Respiratory issues, including asthma or allergies
- Pain and tension in the upper back or shoulder blades
- Prone to illness like bronchitis or pneumonia

BENEFITS OF BALANCE

When our heart chakra is open and balanced, we feel awash with the warmth and acceptance of love. We can give it freely and, just as important, receive it without question or distrust. We make authentic connections and maintain healthy boundaries. The love we have for ourselves is unconditional, and as such our relationships also deepen and become much more profound. The critical chatter in our mind ceases, and forgiveness flows. It brings us to a new level of acceptance for ourselves and for others.

A State of Flow: Bright and beautiful, *anahata* radiates love and acceptance. It allows us to see the interconnectedness of all beings, and teaches us to live from a place of empathy and compassion. We act from a place of love, which ripples into every facet of our existence and every area of our being. We are surrounded and nourished by the life force of love, just as we are always surrounded by its element, air. Such balance brings indescribable joy and also deep peace.

ANAHATA IN HARMONY

With the balancing of our heart chakra comes our first steps towards integrating our physical and spiritual realms, fuelled by love and connection to all. A balanced heart chakra brings:

- Ability to give and receive love
- Acceptance
- Forgiveness, and ability to let go
- Affection
- Empathy
- Compassion
- Connection
- Healthy boundaries
- Healing

HEART CHAKRA AFFIRMATION: 'I LOVE'

The heart chakra's affirmation may be the simplest to comprehend of all the energetic centres. To say it is to know it is to feel it: 'I love'. For more heart chakra affirmations, see page 96.

CRYSTALS

The crystals that connect with the heart chakra are often pink in colour, or green like *anahata* itself. They tend to vibrate with a gentle but powerful feminine energy, opening you up to love. Although the stones below are beneficial for working with this chakra, each addresses a different area of healing with subtle energetic differences.

CHRYSOPRASE

This green stone is a wonderful way to begin work on the heart chakra, especially if you are dealing with heartache or resentfulness. It can help you close the door on that chapter, ushering you in to a new one of happiness, forgiveness and a true feeling of worthiness.

Make some magic: For a clearing, balancing and opening effect, lie down and place a piece of chrysoprase over your heart centre – between your shoulder blades if you are lying face down, or just above your heart if you are on your back. Stay here in meditation for at least several minutes.

GREEN FLUORITE

This is a stone of harmony. Its healing energy focuses on the heart, and can help clear the stagnant energy of past pain while providing a guiding light in all manners of love. It dispels negative energy, so that the path to awakening your heart can be as free as possible.

Make some magic: Meditate with a piece of green fluorite in your hand, for an extra boost of loving support. Try repeating the seed sound for *anahata* (page 96).

PINK TOURMALINE

If you have an underactive heart chakra, pink tourmaline can help. It emanates a gentle nurturing love, and helps open you up to the love of others and yourself, especially if true connection is something you have feared or avoided. It also boosts compassion and empathy.

Make some magic: Keeping a tumbled pink tourmaline in your pocket is like carrying a little love with you at all times. It is a reminder that you are worthy and even more so that we are all connected. Wearing it on a necklace brings it even closer to your heart centre.

ROSE QUARTZ

Rose quartz vibrates with a deep and tender love, supporting the heart through painful transitions and opening it up to genuine self-acceptance. This stone brings an energy of overall rosiness, enhancing connections and strengthening bonds in every area of love.

Make some magic: Keep a piece of rose quartz by your bed so you can end your day with its loving energy, bask in its presence all night and wake each morning to a sense of harmony.

Opposite, clockwise from top: pink tourmaline; chrysoprase; rose quartz; green fluorite

ESSENTIAL OILS

The oils that resonate with the heart chakra evoke a sense of romance, comfort, acceptance and peace. They are floral, herbal and woody too. Here are a few for your *anahata* journey, along with suggestions for use.

OIL	USE
Frankincense[*] The woody, spicy aroma of this ancient, mystical scent is a wonderful mood enhancer, helping to foster a sense of well-being. Steam-distilled from the tree resin of *Boswellia carterii*, it can also address the respiratory issues a heart chakra imbalance may cause.	Diffuse in your home to create a safe, inviting, heart-opening environment.
Jasmine[*] The heady, floral scent of jasmine is well loved and widely used and can be a wonderful oil for gently opening the heart. Extracted from the flowers of *Jasminum officinale*, jasmine oil can also boost your confidence as well as your sense of well-being.	To bring loving awareness to your heart, mix 2 drops jasmine oil with a few drops of carrier oil. Rub onto the skin over the sternum.

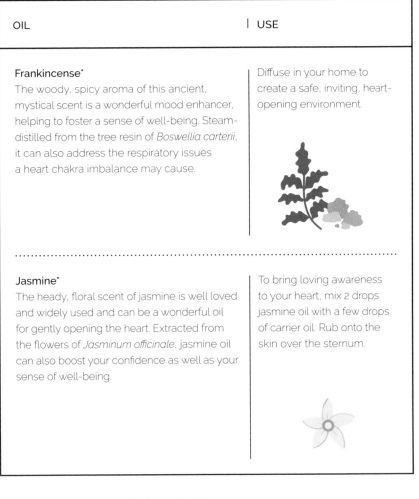

*Do not use while pregnant or breastfeeding
**May irritate sensitive skin

OIL	USE

Marjoram*

Marjoram is commonplace in the kitchen, but the oil from this fragrant herb, *Origanum majorana*, can foster feelings of peace and tranquillity too. It can also be used to address the more physical symptoms of a blocked *anahata*, like poor circulation.

If you suffer cold feet (figurative and literal!), use marjoram to boost your circulation. Add 12 drops marjoram oil to 2 tablespoons carrier oil. Blend and massage into your feet and lower legs.

Palmarosa* **

This sweet, subtle scent has hints of flowers and citrus and provides a reliable emotional uplift. Steam-distilled from the flowering grass *Cymbopogon martinii*, palmarosa oil can be beneficial for skin health too.

For a calming blend, make some smelling salts. Blend 12 drops palmarosa oil with 8 drops lavender and add to 1 tablespoon Epsom salts. Mix and store in a small vial.

Rose

Much like rose quartz emanates love, rose oil – extracted from the fragrant petals of *Rosa damascena* – helps to create a soothing and supportive atmosphere. It can help with all manners of the heart, alleviating depression, tempering any wild emotions you may have and even sparking romance.

For a little self-love and pampering, add rose oil to a face serum and use before you go to bed, an aromatic reminder that you are loved (see page 86).

NOURISHING FACE OIL

This blend is good for the skin and the soul, nourishing the heart chakra.

INGREDIENTS

1 tablespoon jojoba oil
2 teaspoons rosehip oil
5 drops rose essential oil

3 drops frankincense essential oil
2 drops lavender essential oil

Combine all the oils in a small bowl or measuring cup with a spout then pour into a 60 ml (¼ cup) dark blue or amber glass dropper bottle (you can use a small funnel to prevent spillage). At night, rub 1–2 drops between your palms and gently pat over your dry, freshly washed face several times a week. Combine with a heart-opening affirmation for an extra nourishing ritual (see page 96).

FOOD

The heart chakra is all about love, including self-love, and eating healthy is an easily accessible form of self-care – we *have* to make time for meals, so the opportunity to take better care of ourselves is already given to us three times a day. Bitter and astringent foods are associated with air, *anahata*'s element, and anything green aligns with its vibrational colour.

BITTER & ASTRINGENT FOODS

An underactive heart chakra can get a boost from bitter foods and those that have an astringent quality, items that create a dry sensation in your mouth. (If you have ever tasted a dry wine, you know the feeling.)

Leafy greens: Greens like rocket (arugula), kale and spinach are an easy way to add *anahata*-boosting foods to your diet. They are high in iron and fibre as well as vitamins and antioxidants. Enjoying a hearty salad for lunch is a great way to incorporate them.

Dark chocolate: The darker the chocolate, i.e. the higher the cocoa content, the more bitter and astringent it will be. Dark chocolate is also rich in minerals and antioxidants. It is fitting that dark chocolate would support the heart, since it is something we often turn to as a gesture of romance and also a comfort in times of heartache. It makes a wonderful treat.

Pomegranate seeds: Related to the root chakra because of their deep magenta colour, pomegranate seeds are also very astringent, so they can help boost *anahata* as well. The small jewel-like seeds are rich in vitamins, antioxidants and minerals.

GREEN FOODS

Green foods are associated with the vibrant colour of *anahata*, and they happen to be heart-healthy as well. Green foods are packed with chlorophyll, which is rich in vitamins A, C, E and K, and offers minerals and antioxidants too.

Avocados: Full of vitamins and minerals, avocados are perhaps best known for the healthy fats they provide, which can help lower bad cholesterol. They are creamy and satiating and can be added to a wide range of dishes from sweet, like avocado mousse and smoothies, to savoury.

Celery: This vegetable is packed with fibre, antioxidants and minerals, including potassium and folate. Celery also contains vitamins A, C and K, all of which can benefit the cardiovascular system. Snack on it raw, add slices to salads or juice it.

Green fruit: There are many green fruits that can help balance *anahata*, including green apples, kiwi fruit and limes. Each has a number of nutrients and most can be a tasty snack on their own, or added to salads.

Broccoli: These cruciferous florets are packed with nutrients, from B vitamins to folic acid. Studies have also shown that broccoli is good for heart health, lowering the risk of cardiovascular disease.

HERBS & SPICES
These revitalising green herbs are full of heart-opening energy.

Mint: This refreshing herb is anti-inflammatory, full of antioxidants and can also ease digestion. Use it to add some zing to a variety of dishes.

Parsley: This herb is also rich in antioxidants and vitamins, including vitamin K. Parsley can have a detoxifying effect. Add it to soups, salads, egg dishes, pesto or as a garnish for any number of savoury dishes.

DRINK GREEN TEA
Green tea has a number of health benefits, including high levels of antioxidants. Because of its colour and astringency, it is also good for balancing the heart chakra. Turn your daily cup of tea into a ritual, and it can offer the additional benefits of mindful self-care as well (see page 137 for details).

ENJOYING RAW FOOD
Although eating fruits and vegetables in any form is beneficial, many lose their bitter or astringent quality when cooked. If you want to get the full heart-expanding effects of green foods, enjoy them raw.

GREEN JUICE

Bright chartreuse and packed with bitter and astringent leafy greens, this juice has big heart energy.

INGREDIENTS

1–2 green apples, chopped
2 stems of kale, stalks removed
½ lime, peeled

1 large mint sprig

Push all the ingredients through a juicer. Stir to mix together and enjoy.

SHREDDED GREEN SALAD

This major heart-boosting salad also provides a dose of grounding root chakra energy.

INGREDIENTS

1 curly kale leaf, stalk removed
   and leaves thinly sliced
20 g (¾ oz) baby spinach, thinly
   sliced
½ avocado, diced
1 celery stalk, thinly sliced

2 tablespoons chopped parsley
1 tablespoon chopped mint
2 tablespoons pomegranate seeds
salt and pepper
1 tablespoon olive oil
juice of 1 lime

Combine all the vegetables and herbs in a salad bowl. Scatter over the pomegranate seeds, season with salt and pepper and drizzle with olive oil. Add the lime juice and toss to combine.

YOGA POSES

Heart-opening poses can help move energy, offer powerful release and nurture the processing of all kinds of emotions.

ADHO MUKHA SVANASANA
(Downward-facing Dog)

Begin on your hands and knees in a tabletop position – with shoulders above your wrists and your knees hip-width apart. Your middle finger should be facing forward, or you can turn your hands very slightly out, so that the crease of your wrist is parallel with the top of your mat. On an exhalation, tuck your toes under, draw your belly in, push the floor away with your hands and lift your hips up and back, coming into an inverted V. Because the heart chakra governs the hands, pay special attention to them here: spread the fingers and press down with your palms, drawing energy up from the earth. Then open the back of your heart centre by pulling your shoulders down away from your ears and rotating your upper arms out, creating space between the shoulder blades. Lengthen the spine, draw your heels down and hang your head. Stay here for five breaths.

URDVHA MUKHA SVANASANA
(Upward-facing Dog)

From Downward-facing Dog, move through Plank Pose (page 74) to a push-up position. Inhale, press into your hands, straighten your arms and lift your chest keeping your hips up off the mat. Untuck your toes and press the tops of your feet into the mat, engaging the quads and knees to lift them off the floor. Engage your lower belly and tuck your ribcage in. Pull your shoulders back and lift the crown of your head. Gaze straight ahead or gently tilt your head back (keeping the back of your neck long) and gaze towards the ceiling. Stay here for five breaths.

ANJANEYASANA (Low Crescent Lunge)

From Downward-facing Dog step your right foot forward, hands on either side of your foot. Bring your bent knee over your right ankle. Lower your left knee to the ground, untucking your toes. Bring your hands to your knees, lift your chest and drop your tailbone. Raise your arms up overhead, palms facing, chin tilted slightly up and gaze straight ahead. Continue tucking your right hip in and back, pressing into your right foot to lift up and away from your thigh. Stay for five breaths. Return to Downward-facing Dog and repeat on other side.

GARUDASANA (Eagle Pose)

Begin in Mountain Pose (page 34). Bend the knees, lift your right foot and bring your right thigh over the left. Point your right toes and hook them behind your left calf, balancing on the left foot. Extend your arms in front of you, bringing your right arm underneath your left. Bend the elbows so your left elbow is tucked into the bend of the right. Raise your forearms then wrap the forearms so the palms touch. Lift your elbows and stretch your fingers up. Stay for three breaths. Return to Mountain Pose and repeat, switching sides.

SETU BANDHA SARVANGASANA (Bridge Pose)

Lie on your back, knees bent with your feet to the floor, hip-width apart. Rest your arms by your body, palms facing down. With your knees over the ankles, exhale and press your feet into the floor and lift your hips to the ceiling. Draw your tail bone towards the front of the mat. Don't engage your glutes. Roll your shoulders underneath your body and interlace your fingers, drawing your hands towards your heels. Press your arms into the floor and lift your chest. Stay for five breaths. Release your hands. Lower your back to the floor.

VISUALISATION, MEDITATION & AFFIRMATIONS

EXPAND YOUR LOVE

Sit in a comfortable position with your eyes closed. Picture a glowing green sphere spinning in your heart centre. Imagine the glow of that green sphere growing larger and slowing radiating throughout your body. As its light washes over you, feel the love you have for yourself and the divine love the universe has for you. Once your body has been filled with the light, send that love out to your friends and family, then to the people in your community, then to every living being on the planet. See the green energy radiate out from your heart centre connecting you to all of life, a great outpouring of love. Feel that love being seamlessly returned, a constant exchange, enveloping you in its radiant energy. Bring your hands to your heart centre and open your eyes.

Sound Meditation

The seed syllable, or *bija* mantra, for *anahata* is 'yam' (pronounced 'yahhhm'). Chant it slowly, feeling it reverberate in your heart centre. When you are done, see if you can tune in to *anahata*, the unstruck sound, in the silence.

AFFIRMATIONS

Expand your heart centre with affirmations that wash over you with love and acceptance. Use one of the following suggestions, or let them inspire you to create your own personalised affirmation depending on the energy you need. Say it out loud to your reflection in the mirror in the morning and at night, or at the end of a yoga practice. You can also say it silently, whenever you want or need to.

I love myself. I accept myself. I forgive myself.
I am worthy of all the love the universe has to give.
I am surrounded by love, giving and receiving it with an open heart.
I honour the connection of all living things.
I think with compassion, speak with empathy and feel with love.
I give love freely and receive it exponentially.
My heart is strong. My heart is safe.
My heart knows no bounds.
I choose light and joy.
I am one with humanity, with all creatures great and small, and with the earth itself.

RITUALS & ACTIVITIES

Love is all around. The key is to find ways to feel it. The wonderful thing with *anahata* energy is that you can start very small. What may seem insignificant will grow exponentially, until you are filled to the brim with feelings of compassion and acceptance.

Curb self-criticism. Often, the mental chatter in our head can be negative or judgemental without us even realising it. This internal, unchecked criticism can have a detrimental effect on our everyday well-being. The first step is to recognise when you are being unkind to yourself. The next step is to stop the negative chatter when it starts. Once you are in the habit of quelling the negative voice in your head, work on replacing what the voice might typically say with something positive and more affirming. Once the voice in our head is more loving and accepting of us, it naturally becomes kinder to others as well.

Gratitude practice. Focusing on all the things we have, rather than the things we don't, helps create a mindset of abundance rather than lack. This shift in thinking can have a huge effect, and the key is to make it second nature by working a gratitude practice into your daily life. Do this in whatever way works best for you, whether it is writing down three things that you are thankful for every night, recording a voice message when you experience instances of gratitude, or taking a mental note every morning of something you are grateful for. Try to be specific and see how your gratitude grows.

Self-massage. True love begins with the self, and one of the ways we can nurture our body and well-being is with self-massage. Before taking a shower, add a few drops of your favourite heart-opening essential oil to 2 tablespoons carrier oil. Use it to massage your body, using long, steady strokes in the direction of your heart. Include your face, as long as your skin isn't sensitive to the oils you are using, and hands and feet as well. Pair your massage with an affirmation to make the ritual even more powerful. Let the oil soak in for a few minutes, then rinse off.

Volunteer. One way to tap into the infinite love of the universe is by being of service. Choose a cause you feel passionate about and research the different organisations in your area that might have volunteer opportunities. Make room in your schedule to volunteer regularly, in order to build relationships and deepen your connection to the work.

Write love letters. In this day and age, any kind of handwritten correspondence feels special. To write or receive a love letter is even more so. It doesn't have to be romantic. Simply set aside some time to write to the special people in your life, letting them know how much they mean to you.

THROAT CHAKRA

Communication + Authenticity + Self-expression

Overview: The throat chakra is the fifth chakra in our energetic system, and the first of the upper three spiritual chakras, which connect less to our physical being and more to a higher consciousness. It is located at the base of the throat. It governs our ability to know our highest truth and the way in which we are able to speak it.

Sanskrit Name

Vishuddha: In Sanskrit, *shuddhi* means 'pure' and *vi* magnifies it, so *vishuddha* literally translates to 'especially pure'.

The throat chakra represents self-expression, how we communicate, whether or not we are able to speak freely, truthfully and in a manner that lets us be understood. But it also governs what we say. Opening and balancing the lower chakras has laid the foundation for authentic expression. We feel grounded and confident, free to explore life and its wonders. We have connected to the power within, and have filled our heart with love. All of this has prepared us for opening the throat chakra. It allows us to tune in to our deepest desires, trust our intuition and also have faith in the universe. It not only lets us know our truth, but also authentically shares our truth with others. *Vishuddha* governs communication – our ability to voice our wants, relay ideas and express the creativity our sacral chakra helps illuminate. The throat chakra also represents our integrity, the moral compass we follow and uphold. It is a powerful balance of listening and speaking. The throat chakra is the bridge between our heart and our mind, it is our doorway to the divine.

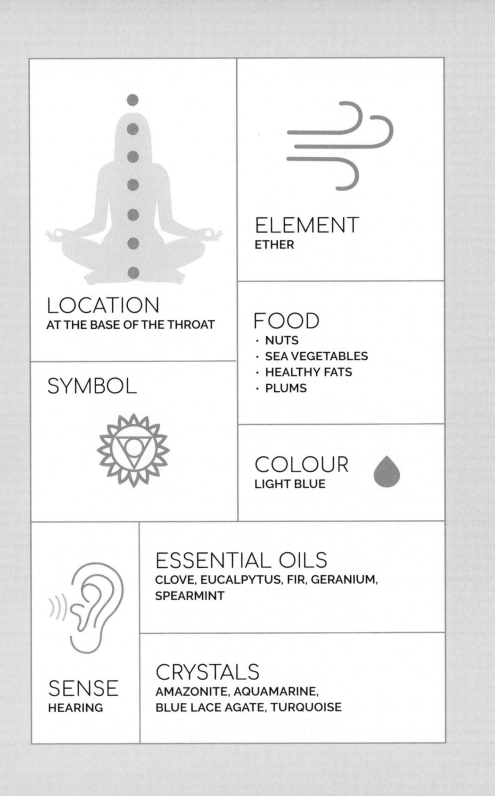

LOCATION
AT THE BASE OF THE THROAT

SYMBOL

ELEMENT
ETHER

FOOD
· NUTS
· SEA VEGETABLES
· HEALTHY FATS
· PLUMS

COLOUR
LIGHT BLUE

SENSE
HEARING

ESSENTIAL OILS
CLOVE, EUCALPYTUS, FIR, GERANIUM,
SPEARMINT

CRYSTALS
AMAZONITE, AQUAMARINE,
BLUE LACE AGATE, TURQUOISE

SYMPTOMS OF IMBALANCE

An out-of-balance throat chakra not only results in challenges to authentic self-expression, but can also make us feel disconnected from our highest truth to begin with, so that we might not even know what kind of authenticity we want to express. Physically, a blocked or overactive *vishuddha* can manifest as ailments in the throat, mouth or even ears.

Overactive Chakra: An overactive throat chakra may mean that our expression is out of control. We may talk too much or too loudly. We may talk over others without ever listening. This applies to our intuition too. If we are too busy talking, we won't be able to hear what our gut is trying to tell us. Our speech, both internal and external, may be non-stop, and with little awareness – critical, judgemental and thoughtless.

Underactive Chakra: An underactive throat chakra is just the opposite. We may be afraid to speak up, silenced by our fear of being judged. We may keep our opinions to ourselves, or be unsure of what our opinions are. We may tell people what they want to hear, rather than what we truly mean. Our inner truth may feel elusive, and our creativity may be blocked.

MENTAL & EMOTIONAL SYMPTOMS

An imbalanced throat chakra can cause a variety of issues related to what we express and how we express it.

- Self-criticism
- Fear of judgement
- Lack of faith
- Inability to articulate needs and desires
- Creatively blocked
- Unable to speak out, or insecure about doing so
- Inauthentic communication with others
- Repression of emotions or dismissive of needs
- Feelings of insignificance or invisibility

PHYSICAL SYMPTOMS

Physical manifestations of a *vishuddha* imbalance tend to surface in the throat and mouth area.

- Sore throat
- Clenched jaw or TMJ (temporomandibular joint dysfunction)
- Problems with the gums or teeth
- Neck pain
- Thyroid issues
- Hearing problems

BENEFITS OF BALANCE

When our throat chakra is open and balanced we are able to express ourselves fully and authentically. We can speak up and share opinions without fearing whether they will be accepted or not. We have a true sense of our deepest-held beliefs and are able to articulate them. We can voice our needs, our desires and our dreams. With this comes a profound sense of being heard and understood. We feel valued and we value the expressions and experiences of others too. We can tap into higher truths, and speak with the love and faith that flows through us. We also speak with the compassion of our heart centre, and with the awareness of interconnectedness guiding our communication.

A State of Flow: A balanced throat chakra also means we are actively listening – to those close to us, to marginalised voices and also to ourselves. We are able to speak up for ourselves and for others who are unable to speak up for themselves. Our heightened intuition leads to a strong gut instinct that we naturally trust and express. We feel creatively free and able to bring our ideas to fruition, which brings with it a great sense of fulfilment. Our ability to communicate openly and honestly, with grace and empathy, strengthens our connections and our pursuit of the greater good.

VISHUDDHA IN HARMONY

Bringing our throat chakra into balance also brings our inner and outer selves into alignment. We speak our truths and act upon them. A balanced throat chakra brings greater:

- Independence
- Intuition
- Expression
- Creativity
- Understanding
- Belonging
- Feelings of value and significance
- Capacity for listening
- Spirituality

THROAT CHAKRA AFFIRMATION: 'I SPEAK'

The affirmation for the throat chakra is 'I speak', the manifestation of what it compels us to do. On the flipside of that is something just as important, the unspoken part of the throat chakra's affirmation: 'I listen'. For more throat chakra affirmations, see page 116.

CRYSTALS

The blue stones of the throat chakra all aid self-expression. Like the chakra itself, their energies bridge the physical and the spiritual. Although the following stones are all beneficial for working with the throat chakra, each addresses a different area of healing with subtle energetic differences.

AMAZONITE

Amazonite is a stone of communication, but it is also a stone of truth. Before it offers support in how to speak authentically, it will help illuminate what it is you want to say. Its ability to bring tranquillity to an overactive mind makes space for clarity and helps to dispel fear. Its manifestation powers work best paired with verbal expression.

Make some magic: Hold a piece of amazonite while voicing your throat chakra–opening affirmations out loud. See page 116 for inspiration.

AQUAMARINE

This beautiful aqua stone resonates deeply with the energy of the throat chakra, especially if you need to clear old habits of silencing your wants and needs. It will help you close that chapter and fearlessly go forward. It is also soothing and can help you attune to your inner knowledge, opening the path towards greater spirituality.

Make some magic: When you sit down to meditate, bring a piece of aquamarine into your sacred space to deepen your inner quiet and help open the door to the divine.

BLUE LACE AGATE

This gentle, soothing stone is especially helpful if working with your throat chakra, bringing up any overwhelming or long-ignored feelings. It can help you navigate the upswell of strong emotions, while giving you access to the right words to voice and process them. It alleviates the fear of being judged, so you can speak your truth.

Make some magic: If you need to have a difficult conversation, keeping a piece of blue lace agate with you can help you find your words.

TURQUOISE

If you feel like years of holding your tongue or having your voice silenced have taken their toll, turn to turquoise. This healing stone can help you release this stagnant or overactive energy, and infuse your path towards balanced self-expression with wisdom and positivity.

Make some magic: For a clearing and balancing effect, lie down facing up and place a piece of turquoise over your throat chakra – at the base of your neck in the nook just above the top of your breastbone, between your collarbones. Meditate for at least several minutes.

Opposite, clockwise from top: aquamarine; turquoise; amazonite; blue lace agate

ESSENTIAL OILS

Most of the oils associated with the throat chakra have an invigorating, sinus-clearing effect to help open the throat and stimulate *vishuddha*. Here are a few woody, spicy, camphorous oils that are great for clearing and boosting throat chakra energy.

OIL	USE
Clove· ·· ··· Sweet and spicy, clove oil is especially good for treating issues with the mouth, including bad breath and gum disease (it is both antiseptic and anti-inflammatory). The oil is distilled from the dried buds of a fragrant tree, *Syzygium aromaticum*, and has been used medicinally throughout the ages.	Use clove oil to boost your mouth health by creating a rinse. The recipe on page 106 can act as an energetic 'clearing of the slate', giving your mouth a fresh start for the authentic truths you will be tapping into.
Eucalyptus· ··· Eucalyptus simultaneously soothes and clarifies, giving your brain a boost while calming mental chatter. Its cooling, camphorous scent comes from the leaves and twigs of *Eucalyptus globulus*, and is beneficial in treating a number of cold symptoms too, including chest and sinus congestion.	For a quick, throat-clearing hit, rub a drop of eucalyptus oil between your palms, cover your nose with your hands and inhale deeply.

·Do not use internally
··Do not use while pregnant or breastfeeding
···Do not use if you have epilepsy or are prone to seizures
····May irritate sensitive skin

OIL	USE

Fir**

The scent of fir can instantly transport you – it is like taking a walk in a dense, luscious forest. Its refreshing scent comes from the needles of the coniferous tree *Abies balsamea*, and helps boost energy too.

Diffuse in the home during the day for extra energy and throat balancing.

Geranium ****

This calming, mood-lifting oil, which smells subtly of roses, comes from the pink and white petals and deep green leaves of the flowering shrub *Pelargonium graveolens*. Geranium is also associated with the heart chakra, so it can help bring that *anahata* compassion to your throat chakra work.

Add 1 drop geranium oil to a couple drops of carrier oil and gently rub into the skin over your throat chakra to help balance and energise it.

Spearmint

This familiar oil is wonderfully sweet and minty, a lovely combination for opening the throat chakra. Steam-distilled from the leaves of *Mentha spicata*, it has a more subtle effect than its sister scent peppermint, but works just as well at relieving congestion and freshening up – both physically and energetically.

To alleviate congestion in the chest or sinuses, while also refreshing your mental state, add 3–5 drops spearmint oil to a bowl of steaming hot water. Place a towel over your head, lean over the bowl and inhale deeply for 1–2 minutes.

CLEARING MOUTH RINSE

Boost mouth health while clearing throat chakra energy.

INGREDIENTS
1 drop clove essential oil
1 drop spearmint essential oil
1 tablespoon water

Add the oils to the tablespoon of water. Swish around in your mouth for 30 seconds and spit out.

FOOD

Now that we are in the upper chakras, the foods associated with each one will have less connection to physical benefits and focus more on the energetic resonance of colour – in this case, blue. But, with the throat chakra, there are also foods that can support the thyroid as well as soothe and nourish the throat.

THYROID-SUPPORTING FOODS

The thyroid, which is governed by the throat chakra, has a far-reaching effect on the body and its systems, producing hormones that affect the metabolism of every cell in the body. The following foods help nourish the tiny organ and support its functions.

Nuts: Protein-packed, good-fat nuts like almonds and cashews are always great options. But for a thyroid-supporting powerhouse, reach for Brazil nuts. They are a good source of iron, which the thyroid also needs, as well as selenium, one of the thyroid's most important minerals.

Sea vegetables: The saltiness of sea vegetables can help support the solar plexus chakra, but it is the iodine content of varieties including nori, kelp and wakame that make them so good for the thyroid and throat chakra. Add them to soups or grain bowls for umami-packed flavour.

Healthy fats: The anti-inflammatory benefits of healthy fats like grass-fed butter, ghee and coconut oil are also good for the thyroid. If you drink coffee, try adding a spoonful of a healthy fat to your morning cup, or cook with them for a little added nourishment.

THROAT-SOOTHING FOODS

Other items that can help support the throat chakra are the kinds of things that comfort us when we have a sore throat. Dishes like warm soups and sauces, or adding raw honey and lemon to warm water or a cup of tea.

BLUE FOODS

Blue foods resonate with the colour of the throat chakra, and though there are not too many in our average diet, the ones that exist pack a healthy punch of antioxidants – like anthocyanins and resveratrol – that help lower inflammation and help boost heart health.

Blueberries & blackberries: These small, juicy fruits are rich in vitamins C and K. They have loads of antioxidants and studies have shown their beneficial effect on lowering blood pressure. Add them to your morning porridge or yoghurt, or eat them as a stand-alone snack.

Plums: These bluish-purple stone fruits are also packed with vitamin C and lots of antioxidants that help protect the body's cells from damage and disease. Sliced plums also make a great topping for porridge and yoghurt and can make a delicious base for sauces and jams.

Blue sweetcorn: Like its yellow counterpart, blue sweetcorn is also high in fibre and B vitamins, as well as essential minerals. But it contains more of the antioxidant anthocyanins along with the essential amino acid lysine. Blue corn flour or fresh blue corn tortillas are a delicious way to include this colourful sweetcorn in your diet.

HERBS & SPICES

Herbal teas, decoctions or even syrups, are a lovely way to nourish and hydrate the throat. The following herbs are especially good when working with *vishuddha*.

Elder: Elder, from the small berries and tiny white flowers of *Sambucus nigra*, is quite the immunity booster, and is good at relieving congestion.

Sage: This tonic herb can help reduce inflammation while it calms the nervous system. It also has been shown to shorten the life of a sore throat.

Thyme: This is another herb with a soothing effect on the throat and respiratory tract. It also makes for a relaxing tonic.

CUT BACK ON DAIRY

If you find yourself suffering from chronic allergies and congestion, which can be manifestations of an imbalanced throat chakra, you could try cutting back on dairy products. Some people experience a reduction in mucus production when eliminating dairy products, which can help clear the throat and the energy of *vishuddha*.

HONEY & LEMON TEA

Soothe your throat with this warming tea.

INGREDIENTS

1 black teabag
200 ml (7 fl oz) water
1 teaspoon honey

1 tablespoon lemon juice
1 lemon slice

Preparation: 5 mins | **Steep time:** 5 mins | **Serves:** 1

Boil the kettle, put the teabag into a mug and pour over the boiling water. Allow the tea to steep for 5 minutes. Remove the teabag, add honey and lemon juice and stir. Serve with a slice of lemon and sip slowly.

FRUIT SALAD WITH COCONUT YOGHURT

A dairy-free option packed with throat chakra–boosting blues and coconut's healthy fats.

INGREDIENTS

2 tablespoons coconut yoghurt

½ pear, sliced into wedges

1 plum, cut into bite-sized pieces

1½ tablespoons blueberries

3 blackberries

1 teaspoon toasted flaked coconut

Put the yoghurt into a serving bowl, then top with the fruit and scatter over the toasted coconut flakes. Serve.

YOGA POSES

Releasing tension from your neck and shoulders and stretching and energising your throat can help balance and open up *vishuddha*.

MARJARYASANA-BITILASANA (Cat-cow Pose)

Come to a tabletop position on your hands and knees, with your shoulders over your wrists and your hips over your knees. Inhale, curve your back so that your sitting bones and chest reach to the ceiling. Tilt your head back to look ahead. Exhale, move through a neutral 'tabletop' position; press into your hands and round your back, arching to the ceiling. Release your head, dropping your chin to your chest. Repeat five times.

SIMHASANA (Lion Pose)

Start in a kneeling position with your buttocks on your feet, palms facing down on your thighs. Inhale, stretching the crown of your head towards the ceiling to lengthen your spine. Open your mouth wide, stick your tongue out and exhale forcefully through your mouth, pushing the air out by contracting your core, and making a roar-like 'haaaaa' sound through the back of your throat. Repeat several times.

SALAMBA SARVANGASANA (Supported Shoulderstand)

Lay on two blankets, folded into a square, with your head on the floor. With your hands on the floor by your hips, come into Plough Pose (right). Rotate your upper arms out rolling onto the edges of the shoulders. Bend your elbows, placing your hands on your lower back. Raise your right leg to the ceiling then raise your left leg to meet it. Walk your hands up your back towards the floor. Pull your elbows in and raise your buttocks up. Stay for five breaths. Return to Plough Pose.

HALASANA (Plough Pose)

From Supported Shoulderstand (left) bend at the hips slowly dropping your feet over and behind your head. Flex your feet so your toes touch the floor. Drop your hands from your back and stretch your arms out along the floor behind you. Clasp your hands together and press the arms into the floor, lifting the backs of your thighs to the ceiling. Stay for five breaths. Unclasp your hands, press your palms into the floor and slowly roll out of Plough Pose.

MATSYASANA (Fish Pose)

Lying on your back, bend your knees, feet to the floor hip-distance apart. With your arms by your body, press into the mat with your feet, and lift your hips keeping your knees hip-width apart. Place your hands palms facing down on the floor underneath your hips. Lower your buttocks onto your hands, and slide each foot to the end of the mat to straighten your legs. With your elbows hugging the side of your body, press into your forearms to lift the chest and shoulders. Drop your head and lower down onto your crown. Engage your legs and press into your palms and elbows. Stay for five breaths. Lift your chest, move your arms to the side and gently lower down.

UJJAYI BREATH

Ujjayi breath is a foundational element of hatha yoga practice. Close your mouth, inhaling and exhaling steadily through your nose. Begin to deepen your breath. On the next exhalation, gently constrict your throat muscles, making an 'ocean' sound. Continue inhaling and exhaling through your nose, keeping your length of breath consistent and allowing the sound to support your internal rhythm when seated and your movement when practising *asanas*.

VISUALISATION, MEDITATION & AFFIRMATIONS

SHARE YOUR TRUTH

Sit in a comfortable position. Add 1 drop eucalyptus oil to 1 drop carrier oil, and rub it into the skin over your throat chakra. Close your eyes and begin to deepen your breath. As you breathe, follow your breath as it comes in through your nose, down your throat, into the lungs and then the belly. Do this for several breaths. On the next breath, picture a glowing blue sphere where your throat chakra is. As your breath passes through your throat chakra, imagine it takes on the blue light of the sphere, carrying that light into your chest and your belly. With each inhalation, the blue light expands, upward and downward, until your body is filled. As you exhale, breathe out the energy of past negative patterns, releasing any feelings of guilt. On your last three breaths, imagine being filled with the blue light. Sit for a few breaths then open your eyes.

Sound Meditation

The seed syllable, or *bija* mantra, for *vishuddha* is 'ham' (pronounced 'hahhhm'). Draw it out feeling the sound vibrate in your throat chakra.

AFFIRMATIONS

Engage and honour the power of your voice, and the power of your quiet to help balance your throat chakra. Use one of the following suggestions, or let them inspire you to create your own personalised affirmation depending on the energy you need. Say it out loud to your reflection in the mirror in the morning and at night, or at the end of a yoga practice. You can also say it silently, whenever you want or need to.

I am free to speak my truth.

I am heard, understood and valued.

I know my truth. I speak my truth. I embody my truth.

I advocate for myself, and for others whose voices are not being heard.

I speak with compassion, empathy and love.

I listen with patience; I listen without judgement.

My intuition is strong and I trust it wholeheartedly.

I am confident in my creativity and feel passionate about expressing it.

My voice is powerful and I use it wisely.

Through clear communication I strengthen my connections.

RITUALS & ACTIVITIES

Finding your voice, seeing the power in silence and getting in touch with your inner truths are all part of the path towards balancing your throat chakra.

Sing out loud. Sometimes learning to sing can help teach you how to speak. Wake your throat chakra up by taking the song in your head and singing it out loud. Maybe it is just in the shower, or humming while you go about your day. Maybe karaoke is something you have been wanting to do. It doesn't matter where, when or how, just warm up those vocal chords and get comfortable singing out loud.

Bathe in sound. Since sound is the sense we associate with the throat chakra, and it is *vishuddha* that governs the ears, luxuriating in a sound bath can help loosen stagnant emotions and get energy flowing in a whole new way.

Try journalling. If you don't already do so, regularly writing your innermost thoughts down on paper can be an illuminating way to get in touch with your authenticity and sort through all the mental chatter and emotions in your head. Try keeping a journal every day for a week, and just observe what comes up as you write. Sometimes, the act of simply writing something out, as opposed to typing it, can help us understand it or integrate it in a way that isn't accessible through technology.

Appreciate blue skies. In the non-stop busyness of our everyday lives, we don't often look up enough. But when we do we are greatly rewarded, especially on a clear day, by a great expanse of bright blue sky. Take an afternoon to slow down and enjoy it, lying on your back on a blanket in your garden or a park, watching as the clouds drift by. The sky's azure hue resonates with the colour of *vishuddha*, and you will be steeping yourself in ether, the throat chakra's corresponding element.

Enjoy the silence. As much as authentic self-expression is a hallmark of the throat chakra, when this energy centre is balanced, staying quiet becomes just as powerful and insightful. Not only in conversation with others, giving you a chance to listen and connect, but also with yourself, so you can slow down and hear what your inner voice is trying to tell you. If you have an overactive throat chakra and are not used to quiet, sitting in silence can be quite uncomfortable. But with a little practice, you will come to find the absence of sound is actually quite nourishing. Take up a silent meditation practice, or simply raise your awareness about how you use sound to fill the void, and be mindful of using it only with intention.

THIRD EYE CHAKRA

Intuition ◆ Higher Wisdom ◆ Harmony

Overview: The third eye chakra, also called the brow chakra, is the sixth chakra in our energetic system. It is located on the forehead, between our eyebrows. It is home to our intuition and the 'eye' with which we see beyond the physical realm. It is the mind centre that brings together our intuition and intellect, to broaden our curiosity and understanding of existence. It is where we deepen our well of wisdom and open ourselves to guidance – inner and divine.

Sanskrit Name
Ajna: *Ajna* generally translates to 'perceive' or 'beyond wisdom'.

If the throat chakra is the bridge between the heart and the mind, the doorway to the divine, our third eye chakra is where we are able to fully explore and expand into a higher state of consciousness. It raises our awareness to a whole new level of vibration. *Ajna* is where we attune to and develop our intuition, where we reconnect with our inner guide that draws from energy beyond our physical body in order to enhance our insight and light our path. The third eye chakra is where we learn to trust that which we cannot hear, touch, smell, taste or see with our physical eyes, but what we can sense with our inner being, what we can 'see' with our mind's eye. It integrates these two ways of knowing, so that we can remain wholly present while our capacity for understanding exponentially expands. *Ajna* provides us with a deep inner trust. We trust our intuition, we trust our path, we trust that all things are as they should be. This energetic flow floods us with a sense of true harmony, radiating out and lighting up the whole of our interconnectedness.

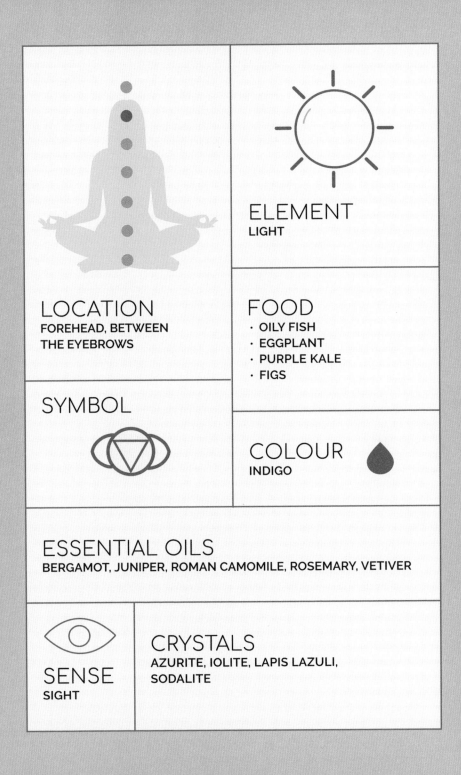

LOCATION
FOREHEAD, BETWEEN
THE EYEBROWS

SYMBOL

ELEMENT
LIGHT

FOOD
· OILY FISH
· EGGPLANT
· PURPLE KALE
· FIGS

COLOUR
INDIGO

ESSENTIAL OILS
BERGAMOT, JUNIPER, ROMAN CAMOMILE, ROSEMARY, VETIVER

SENSE
SIGHT

CRYSTALS
AZURITE, IOLITE, LAPIS LAZULI,
SODALITE

SYMPTOMS OF IMBALANCE

A third eye chakra that is out of balance can lead to feelings of disconnection, distrust of our intuition and all of the problems that come with being too much 'in our head'. Physically it governs our pineal gland, as well as our sight and sinuses and the lower part of our brain.

Overactive Chakra: Although it is rare to experience an overactive third eye chakra, it is possible, especially if you begin to open your third eye without bringing the lower chakras into balance. An overactive *ajna* can mean you are out of touch with reality, indulging in fantasies and daydreams without any sense of grounding. You may also feel like you are being bombarded with visions and dreams, getting swept up without the ability or stability to properly receive and process the information.

Underactive Chakra: In our modern times, when our reality is grounded in the physical world and we constantly rely on and are bombarded with technology, a blocked third eye chakra is much more common. We may feel cut off from our intuition. We may distrust our gut or ignore our inner voice. Our realm of thought may feel very narrow and limiting, and we might be fearful or resistant to the idea of expanding it. We might feel like our life lacks meaning, or a greater purpose. We may have an inkling that there is something more to this existence, but we just cannot access the bigger picture.

MENTAL & EMOTIONAL SYMPTOMS

When our third eye chakra is out of alignment, the result is a lack of inner guidance, and the toll it can take mentally, emotionally and spiritually.

- Disconnected from our intuition
- General dissatisfaction
- Lack of meaning
- Feelings of being overwhelmed
- Overthinking
- Trouble making decisions
- Inability to concentrate
- Poor memory

PHYSICAL SYMPTOMS

An imbalanced third eye chakra can be tied to several physical symptoms as well.

- Headaches
- Insomnia or nightmares
- Issues with vision
- Hormonal disorders related to the pituitary gland

BENEFITS OF BALANCE

When our third eye is open, we no longer rely only on our physical senses for information. Our perception cracks open, we see the beauty and magic and energetic connection in everything. We are no longer tethered by the limited knowledge of what is right in front of us. We are acutely aware and tuned in to ourselves, to our surroundings and to those around us. We use all of the information we receive to make decisions with certainty. At the same time, we don't feel overly attached to the outcome, we simply see things as they are, not as we want them to be.

A State of Flow: Clearing and opening our third eye chakra, helps us vibrate on a higher level, regarding others with the same open-mindedness we have found in ourselves. We lead with curiosity and acceptance, not judgement or criticism. We can be wholly present, experiencing the world with a much wider perspective, .rather than the narrow viewpoint of the self. A balanced *ajna* fosters our sense of love and acceptance, of interconnectedness and harmony. We can see clearly now.

AJNA IN HARMONY

To effectively work on opening our third eye chakra, we must do the work of bringing the lower chakras into balance. This provides the grounding and stability that allows us to access our ability to truly 'see'. A balanced third eye chakra brings greater:

- Intuition
- Awareness
- Inner guidance
- Emotional intelligence
- Self-assuredness
- Decision-making capabilities
- Trust
- Harmony
- Empowerment

> ### THIRD EYE CHAKRA AFFIRMATION: 'I SEE'
> The third eye chakra allows us to trust beyond what's right in front of us, beyond our limited experience. When we open our third eye chakra, we can truly say, 'I see'. For more third eye chakra affirmations, see page 136.

CRYSTALS

The crystals that resonate with our third eye chakra reconnect us with our intuition, support our spiritual awareness and open us up to new ways of seeing. Though the following stones are all beneficial for working with the third eye chakra, each addresses a different area of healing with subtle energetic differences.

AZURITE

Also known as a 'stone of heaven', azurite helps boost our connection to the divine, making us more receptive to what is true and aware of what may be. Azurite is also a stone of perspective, gently supporting new ways of seeing as it encourages us to let go of limited ways of thinking that no longer serve us.

Make some magic: Keep a piece of azurite on your altar or nightstand as you work on bringing *ajna* into alignment.

IOLITE

The deep blue of iolite can be an energetic guiding light – it can raise our awareness, expand our vision, sharpen our understanding and help connect us to a higher consciousness. It gently vibrates with harmonious positivity. If you are having trouble reconnecting with your intuition, use iolite to come back to yourself.

Make some magic: Meditate with a piece of iolite in your hand, to help quiet your thinking mind and raise the volume of your inner voice.

LAPIS LAZULI

Lapis lazuli is a perfect stone for clearing the third eye chakra as you begin your *ajna* journey. Its energy is that of truth and knowledge – it will inspire you to want to look beyond what you know and seek answers and perspectives outside of yourself. It can also boost your connection to the divine.

Make some magic: Before you begin work on your third eye chakra, lie on your back and place a piece of lapis lazuli on your forehead in between your brows to activate and inspire your journey.

SODALITE

Once your journey towards opening your third eye has begun, use sodalite to deepen the work and make sure your energy is kept in balance. Sodalite has the power to awaken your insight, while keeping your feet rooted to the ground.

Make some magic: Raise the vibration of a blend made from third eye chakra–supporting essential oils (see page 126) by adding small pieces of sodalite to the bottle that holds the mixture.

Opposite, clockwise from top: azurite; iolite; sodalite; lapis lazuli

ESSENTIAL OILS

The oils that resonate with the third eye chakra all support the strengthening of our intuition and connecting with the divine. They range between energising and soothing, floral and herbal – representative of the balance *ajna* requires.

OIL	USE
Bergamot* Citrusy, floral, sweet and spicy, this layered scent can boost a number of chakras including the third eye. Cold pressed from the rinds of *Citrus bergamia*'s fruit, this oil calms while it uplifts, priming our third eye chakra for expanded perception.	Combine bergamot with a carrier oil and use as a roll-on scent whenever you need to feel an embodied sense of happiness (see page 126).
Juniper** *** The fresh, sweet, woody scent of juniper is a mindfulness boon. The oil, distilled from the needles and berries of *Juniperus communis*, has a wonderfully grounding effect, while also awakening the senses.	Before you meditate, mix 1 drop juniper oil with 1 drop carrier oil, and use your finger to dab the mixture on to each of your temples.

*Do not use on skin that may be exposed to the sun
**Do not use while pregnant or breastfeeding
***Do not use if you have kidney or liver ailments
****Do not use if you have epilepsy or are prone to seizures

OIL	USE

Roman Camomile**

This sweet and floral oil has an incredibly calming effect. It soothes the nervous system, allowing you to disengage from your thinking mind and sink into a space of heightened quiet and intuition. Steam-distilled from the tiny flowers of *Anthemis nobilis*, camomile oil also promotes restful sleep, helping to open the channels of communication with our subconscious.

For a soothing bath at the end of the day that will help prepare your body for sleep and your mind for dreaming, add 5 drops camomile oil to 1 tablespoon carrier oil and add to your warm water.

Rosemary** ****

Rosemary's mind-clearing, clarifying capacities are wonderful for easing overthinking or quieting a critical inner monologue. Its slightly sweet, herbal smell comes from the flowering tops of *Rosmarinus officinalis*, and can help you be more present in the moment.

To clear stale energy, diffuse rosemary in the home. Blend it with bergamot to add a dose of emotional uplift.

Vetiver

Vetiver is another oil that's good for the third eye chakra, because it is deeply relaxing while also boosting concentration, helping to clear the path for connection with your inner guide. Distilled from the roots of the grass *Vetiveria zizanioides*, the woody, earthy scent also has a grounding effect.

Add a couple of drops of vetiver to your pillowcase to soothe night-time anxieties and support a restful sleep.

THIRD EYE–OPENING ROLL-ON

This layered blend will boost your senses while deeply calming your body.

INGREDIENTS

3 drops bergamot essential oil

6 drops juniper essential oil

2 drops vetiver essential oil

jojoba oil

small pieces of sodalite (optional)

Preparation: 5 mins | **Storage time:** 6 months | **Storage container:** 10 ml (¼ fl oz) glass roller bottle

Create a blend that will energise, soothe and help you connect with your intuition. Because it is in roll-on form, you can keep this blend with you at all times. Roll on your third eye chakra before meditation, roll on your temples before yoga or roll on your inner wrists when you want to tune in to your inner voice. Place the essential oils and sodalite, if using, in the roller bottle and top with jojoba oil. Swish to combine. If using a clear bottle, keep out of direct sunlight.

FOOD

Foods that support brain health, as well as foods that resonate with the third eye chakra's deep indigo colour, can all help to balance and support *ajna* energy.

BRAIN FOODS
Support your third eye chakra with brain-boosting foods full of omega-3 fatty acids and antioxidants.

Oily fish: If you include fish in your diet, eating those with high concentrations of omega-3 fatty acids are great for brain health. Opt for salmon, sardines or anchovies. Pair a pescatarian main with a side of purple veggies for an *ajna*-boosting meal.

Dark chocolate: Its elemental attributes make dark chocolate good for the heart, but studies have shown that its high content of flavonoids can have a positive cognitive effect. Use cocoa or cacao powder when cooking or baking, sprinkle cocoa nibs on porridge or in smoothies, and when eating chocolate in bar form, opt for one with the highest percentage of cocoa.

PURPLE FOODS
There are lots of purplish-blue foods that energetically resonate with the third eye chakra. Much like the blue foods that support the throat chakra, they are rich in antioxidants – like anthocyanins and resveratrol – that in addition to boosting heart health, are good for the brain as well.

Eggplant (aubergine): This vegetable is especially good for those trying to cut meat out of their diet, thanks to its similarly satisfying hearty texture. It is also high in vitamins C, K and B6 as well as magnesium, potassium and folic acid. It makes a great vegetarian main meal.

Purple kale: This kale has the same nutrient-dense make-up as green kale, packed with vitamins C and K as well as antioxidants. But its purple colour resonates energetically with the third eye chakra, and has a less bitter, more delicate flavour than its heart-supporting counterpart.

Purple grapes: Although grapes are healthy, containing lots of vitamins and minerals, Concord grapes have a higher percentage of flavonoids and brain-boosting antioxidants.

Purple cabbage & cauliflower: Much like purple grapes offer a greater amount of antioxidants than green, so too do the purple versions of cabbage and cauliflower. These cruciferous vegetables are great additions to salads, stir-fries and numerous sides.

Figs: These small, seed-filled purple fruits are perfect for healthily satisfying a sweet tooth. Plus they are packed with vitamins and minerals. Eat them fresh on salads or yoghurt, or just as they are, skin and all.

HERBS & SPICES

The herbs associated with third eye energy both soothe and stimulate, quieting the body and boosting the mind.

Lavender: This herb's purple flowers vibrate with third eye chakra energy. Lavender is also soothing, helping to calm anxiety and promote a good night's sleep.

Mugwort: This herb has been used throughout history to boost intuition. Drink a cup of mugwort tea in the evening, or tuck a mugwort-filled sachet in your pillowcase to welcome vivid dreams.

Rosemary: Much like rosemary essential oil is good for mental clarity, the herb itself is known as a brain tonic, boosting memory and mental acuity.

MINDFUL EATING

Bringing our attention inwards and raising awareness has as much to do with the way we prepare and eat food as it does with the kinds of foods that we eat. Mindful eating is a nourishing practice when raising your chakra vibrations, and it is especially relevant for balancing *ajna*. Mindful eating starts long before the food reaches your plate. Shop locally and seasonally if you can. Carry that attention into the kitchen, prepping and cooking your food with love and awareness. Enjoy the process, savour the smells, sounds and feelings, and go through the motions with a calm peacefulness. When you sit down to eat, close your eyes, inhale and open them. Take your time chewing, and be present with your food. Pay attention to your body, it will let you know when it is satiated. The more often you eat mindfully, the more connected you will feel to eating intuitively.

CACAO & BERRY SMOOTHIE

This third eye chakra–enhancing indigo drink is also packed with brain-boosting cacao.

INGREDIENTS

150 ml (5 fl oz) almond milk

4–5 ice cubes

35 g (1¼ oz) frozen blueberries

1 teaspoon açai berry powder

2 teaspoons raw cacao powder

1 tablespoon maple syrup

Combine all the ingredients in a blender and blend until smooth. Serve and enjoy.

LAVENDER TEA

Bring third eye clarity with this soothing tea.

INGREDIENTS
1 teaspoon dried or fresh lavender

1 rosemary sprig

1 teaspoon agave syrup

Fill a mug with boiling water. Add the lavender (in a tea ball if you have one) and allow to steep in the water for 5 minutes. Add the rosemary sprig and steep for another 1–2 minutes. Remove the tea ball or strain the water and stir in the agave syrup to sweeten. Drink warm or leave to cool and drink over ice for a summer refreshment.

YOGA POSES

The poses associated with *ajna* are all about drawing inwards and stimulating the third eye. They are also about seeing the world from a new perspective, with side twists, inversions and both standing and sitting poses.

BADDHA VIRABHADRASANA
(Humble Warrior Pose)

Begin by moving into Warrior I (page 74) from Mountain Pose (page 34). After several breaths, slide the foot of your bent leg out a few centimetres, release your arms and interlace your fingers behind your back. Draw your shoulders away from your ears, inhale to look up and broaden the chest, drawing your interlaced hands down to the ground. On the exhalation, gently move forward with a flat back bringing your torso to the inside of your bent knee. Press your shoulder against your bent knee, while creating resistance with your bent knee. Keep your hips squared to the front of the mat as you lower your head. Stay for five breaths then slowly come up, returning to Warrior I. Repeat for the other side.

PARIVRTTA PRASARITA PADOTTANASANA
(Wide-legged Forward Fold with a Twist)

From Mountain Pose step your legs out wide, facing the long side of your mat, feet parallel. Come into Wide-legged Forward Fold (page 54), hands to the ground, and stay for several breaths. On an inhalation, lift to a flat back and move your right hand to the centre of the mat. As you exhale, slowly twist your body to the left, bringing your left arm up, fingers to the sky. Turn your head and gaze to the left. Stay for five breaths, then return to Wide-legged Forward Fold and repeat on the other side.

ARDHA PINCHA MAYURASANA (Dolphin Pose)

Begin by taking a few breaths in Downward-facing Dog (page 94). Kneel, bringing your knees to the mat. Bring your forearms to the ground – palms facing down, fingers spread – parallel and shoulder-width apart. Bring your knees under your hips, hugging your upper arms in. Exhale, press your forearms into the ground to lift your hips. Keep your shoulders over your elbows. Release your head so your neck is long. Stay for five breaths, then lower down to your knees.

AGNISTAMBHASANA (Double Pigeon Pose)

Begin in a straight-legged seated position, feet towards the front of your mat. Sit up straight. Lift your chest slightly and pull your shoulders back. Bend your right knee and draw your right foot in, sliding it under your left knee so your shin is parallel to the top of the mat. Bend your left knee and stack your left leg on top of the right, shins parallel, knee over ankle and ankle over knee. Flex both feet. Stay if the hips are tight, or slowly fold forward, walking your hands out in front of you, lengthening your spine as you bring your head down. Stay for five breaths and come up. Unfold your legs, return to a straight-legged seated position. Repeat on the other side.

VISUALISATION, MEDITATION & AFFIRMATIONS

THE POWER OF BREATH

Alternate-nostril breathing is a form of pranayama that brings balance to the system while activating the third eye chakra. Sit in a comfortable position, with your hands resting on your thighs. Hold your right hand in front of your face and press your index and middle finger to your third eye chakra. Bring your thumb and your ring finger to either side of your nose. Close your eyes and press your thumb to your right nostril, blocking the air passage. Inhale through your left nostril, breathing into your third eye at the top of the breath. Release your thumb, close your left nostril with your ring finger and exhale through your right nostril. Inhale through your right nostril, breathing into your third eye at the top of the breath. Release your finger, press your thumb to your right nostril and exhale through your left nostril. Repeat for several minutes. After your last exhale through your left nostril, release the right hand, inhale through both nostrils and exhale. Open your eyes.

Sound Meditation

The seed syllable, or *bija* mantra, for *ajna* is 'om' (pronounced 'auummm'). Chant it slowly while focusing on your third eye chakra, feeling the sound reverberate out through the rest of your body.

AFFIRMATIONS

Deepen your intuition and broaden your mind with affirmations that connect to your inner guide and the greater good. Use one of the following suggestions, or let them inspire you to create your own personalised affirmation depending on the energy you need. Say it out loud to your reflection in the mirror in the morning and at night, or at the end of a yoga practice. You can also say it silently, whenever you want or need to.

I trust and honour my inner wisdom.
My mind is clear and my body is listening.
My feet are rooted and my third eye is open.
I am curious and open-minded.
I am connected to my intuition; I can hear it loud and clear.
I am open to receiving wisdom from without and within.
I am constantly seeking, learning, loving and growing.
I can see the big picture and I trust my place in it.
It is not me and you, but collectively us.

RITUALS & ACTIVITIES

There are many different ways to tune in to your inner voice, open up to divine guidance and expand your perspective. Let your intuition guide you.

Meditate. One of the simplest ways to begin engaging your third eye is through mindfulness meditation. If you have never done it before, start small. Sit in a comfortable position in a quiet space. You can use an essential oil to prepare, or bring a crystal nearby to raise the vibrations. Set a timer for two minutes. Close your eyes and focus on your breath, feeling it enter your body on the inhalation, and leave on the exhalation. If your mind wanders, bring it back to your breath. Continue doing this until your timer goes off, then gently open your eyes.

Be mindful. If seated meditation sounds undesirable to you, never fear. Almost any action can become a meditation if you apply mindfulness to it. You may be washing up, cooking or taking a bath. Infuse the activity with mindfulness by bringing your awareness to your breath. Follow your breath in, and follow it out. If your mind wanders, bring it back to your breath. Doing so will bring you into your body and alive in the present moment.

Honour your circadian rhythm. The third eye chakra governs our pineal gland, which regulates our circadian rhythm and therefore our sleep – a main element of our overall well-being. In modern culture, when so much of our time is spent indoors, we tend to lose touch with our rhythm. Reconnect by exposing yourself to natural light every day: sit by a sunny window or take a walk. Limit the artificial light you are exposed to, and try not to spend time in windowless rooms during the day. Try to adjust your sleep schedule to coincide with the rising and setting of the sun, shifting as the seasons change. Dim the lights and ditch the screens an hour before bedtime.

Start a dream journal. When you begin clearing and energising your third eye chakra, you may begin to dream more. This is your deeper consciousness rising up, connecting your waking life to your innermost workings. Dreams can be full of insight and illumination. The more we pay attention to them the more vivid they become, and the more we begin to understand what they have to teach us. Leave a notebook and pen by your bed. When you wake up, jot down what you can remember. The more you do it, the easier this will become. Notice any patterns or themes that come up.

Seek out opposing viewpoints. Be intentional about exposing yourself to differing viewpoints. Listen to a podcast about something you disagree with, or read articles that differ ideologically from your beliefs. Observe, educate yourself and let go.

CROWN CHAKRA

Unity + Serenity + Divinity

Overview: The crown chakra is the seventh and last of the primary chakras. It is located at the crown of the head. It is our consciousness, our connection to the divine. It propels us to a higher state of being, one of ease, flow, spirit and unity.

Sanskrit Name
Sahasrara: *Sahasrara* translates to 'thousand-petalled', representing the full blooming of higher consciousness.

Sahasrara governs our energetic life. It is the source of our inner wisdom, the channel through which we communicate with the divine. The crown chakra acts as the bridge between our physical and spiritual selves. Unlike the other chakras, it is not associated with a sense, it is merely pure light, energised by thought, the highest level of consciousness. It is what paves our path with purpose. It is what shows us that we are part of a greater whole, that we are spiritual beings living a human experience. The crown chakra governs how we live in life – our presence and awareness and whether we are able to see the beauty and divinity in everything. It reveals the interconnectedness of all things, or, if it is blocked, we may be blind to the way the actions of one can affect the whole. The crown chakra teaches us that our existence expands beyond the physical realm; it is the gateway to a truly higher consciousness. In that sense, it is the chakra that governs the entirety of our well-being.

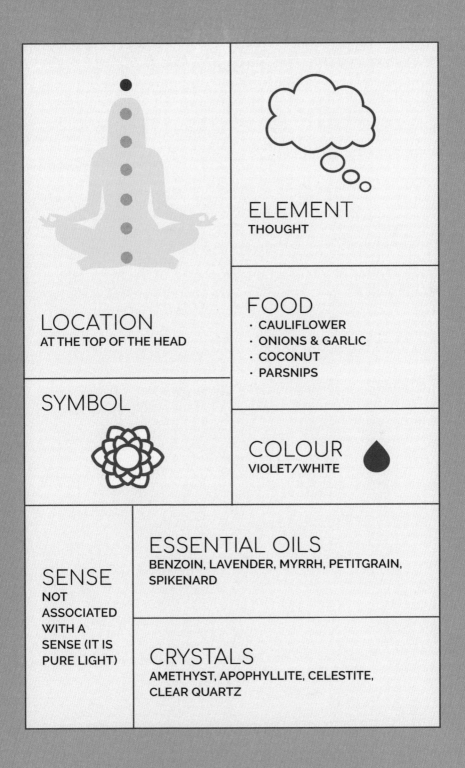

ELEMENT
THOUGHT

FOOD
· CAULIFLOWER
· ONIONS & GARLIC
· COCONUT
· PARSNIPS

LOCATION
AT THE TOP OF THE HEAD

SYMBOL

COLOUR
VIOLET/WHITE

SENSE
NOT
ASSOCIATED
WITH A
SENSE (IT IS
PURE LIGHT)

ESSENTIAL OILS
BENZOIN, LAVENDER, MYRRH, PETITGRAIN,
SPIKENARD

CRYSTALS
AMETHYST, APOPHYLLITE, CELESTITE,
CLEAR QUARTZ

SYMPTOMS OF IMBALANCE

When our crown chakra is blocked or out of alignment, it can affect our well-being. To be disconnected from our higher self causes disconnection from everything.

Overactive Chakra: An overactive crown chakra can make our mind spin out of control. We may fixate or obsess over something, unable to see a broader perspective. It could manifest as an insatiable need for material things, a self-indulgence that disconnects us from the greater good and fuels us with imagined superiority over others.

Underactive Chakra: An underactive crown chakra will make us feel disconnected – from our spiritual self, from other humans and from the world at large. We may feel like life has been drained of colour, or that we are simply watching ourselves go through the motions of life. We may feel a lack of purpose, or that our existence has no greater meaning.

MENTAL & EMOTIONAL SYMPTOMS

An imbalanced crown chakra blocks the flow of energy between our physical self and our higher consciousness, leading to life on a low vibration.

- Apathy
- Loneliness and depression
- Lack of purpose
- Disconnection
- Restlessness and impatience
- Self-centredness
- Obsessive thoughts
- Lack of inspiration
- Narrow-mindedness

PHYSICAL SYMPTOMS

Since the crown chakra governs our energy dispersion, it can manifest in ways that affect the physical body as a whole.

- Fatigue
- Hypersomnia or insomnia
- Brain fog
- Headaches or migraines
- Hormonal issues

BENEFITS OF BALANCE

When our crown chakra is in alignment it is as though we have opened ourselves up to the secrets of the universe and the universe has provided. Our life has purpose and we feel a deeper sense of meaning. We are able to see the divine in the everyday. We act from a place of integrity and interconnectedness. Mind and spirit are aligned – a true sense of elevated harmony.

A State of Flow: Bringing energy to the crown chakra is the culmination of tending to all of the other energy centres that come before it. We have built a strong foundation, rooting us to the earth. We have given our emotions a safe and supported home. We have found our path and embraced our self-worth. We have opened our heart, leading with love, and we have connected with our authentic self, finding the balance between listening and self-expression. We have opened our third eye and learned to 'see'. Now we get to deepen our connection to the divine, to live a spiritual existence in the physical realm, to truly understand the interconnectedness of all life and to let that understanding be the force that guides us.

SAHASRARA IN HARMONY

Bringing awareness to our crown relies on balanced energy in all six chakras that come before it, building the ladder to our higher consciousness. A balanced crown chakra brings greater:

- Love
- Empathy
- Kindness
- Purpose
- Peace
- Faith
- Connection
- Beauty
- Awakening

CROWN CHAKRA AFFIRMATION: 'I KNOW'

The crown chakra's affirmation represents the bridge that *sahasrara* builds between the physical realm and the spiritual one, and the understanding that it brings: 'I know'. For more crown chakra affirmations, see page 156.

CRYSTALS

The clear and violet crystals associated with the crown chakra all hum with the highest vibrations. They are physical portals to the spiritual realm. Although the following stones are all beneficial for working with the crown chakra, each addresses a different area of healing with subtle energetic differences.

AMETHYST

This violet stone vibrates with pure peace and tranquillity. Amethyst will soothe the mind, relax the body and help open the path to spirituality, fostering connection to a higher consciousness. It can also help ease insomnia if that is one of your manifestations of imbalance.

Make some magic: Use small pieces of amethyst to infuse and boost the vibrations of a crown chakra–clearing essential oil spray (see page 146).

APOPHYLLITE

Apophyllite will help you put in the work it takes to clear, stimulate and open the crown chakra. It is a stone of illumination – granting you deep awareness to understand the changes you must make, while reminding you of the interconnectedness of all life. Its calming energy brings the mind and spirit together.

Make some magic: Hold a piece of apophyllite while you meditate to drop deeper in to your inner wisdom, gain insight into behaviours and patterns that need work and help foster your connection to the divine.

CELESTITE

There is a reason celestite is known as a stone of heaven – it vibrates with energy on a higher plane. If scepticism and disconnection are things that you struggle with, you will find comfort and clarity in this pale blue crystal. It will open you up to the truth of existence, offering insight into your place in the universe and the deep inner peace that comes with that knowing.

Make some magic: Keep a piece of celestite by your bed. Its tranquil energy is perfect for promoting sleep and it can also enhance your dreams.

CLEAR QUARTZ

This stone is full of light – let its aura of positivity and purification wash over your energetic body. Its incredibly supportive properties can tune up all your chakras, bringing them into balance before clearing a path for the crown chakra to flourish, fostering a connection to higher consciousness.

Make some magic: Lie down and place a piece of clear quartz on the floor above the crown of your head. Meditate on its ability to cleanse and align all the chakras.

Opposite, clockwise from top: clear quartz; celestite; amethyst; apophyllite

ESSENTIAL OILS

The heady fragrances associated with the crown chakra offer intoxicating aromas and deep relaxation. Here are a few that are great for clearing the mind of anxieties and opening the door to the divine.

OIL	USE
Benzoin The warm, vanilla-like scent of this woody oil is deeply calming and comforting. Extracted from the resin of the white-blossomed tree *Styrax tonkinensis*, benzoin oil is also known for aiding insomnia.	Diffuse near your bed at night to help promote restful sleep. Blends well with jasmine or sandalwood for an especially intoxicating scent.
Lavender Lavender can be beneficial for all of the energy centres, but works especially well with the crown chakra. Steam-distilled from the flowering tops of *Lavandula angustifolia* (it resonates on a colour level as well), its fresh floral scent is good for promoting calmness as well as treating headaches.	To treat a headache, mix 2 drops lavender oil with 2 drops carrier oil and rub the mixture onto each temple, inhaling deeply.

*May irritate sensitive skin
**Do not use internally
***Do not use while pregnant or breastfeeding

OIL	USE

Myrrh ** ***
This healing oil has a long history of mysticism and spirituality. Steam-distilled from the resin of *Commiphora myrrha*, myrrh has a warm, spicy, enveloping scent, well known for its ability to deeply calm the nerves.

To bring awareness, mix 1 drop myrrh with 1 drop carrier oil. Apply to your crown before meditating.

Petitgrain
The floral, woody, citrusy scent of petitgrain works wonders on the body, calming emotions, reducing anxiety and aiding rest. Petitgrain – neroli's sister oil – is distilled from the leaves and twigs of *Citrus aurantium*, and can also treat muscle spasms and skin flare-ups.

Blend petitgrain with other crown chakra–stimulating oils to create a *sahasrara* spray (see page 146) that can be used before bed, meditation and yoga.

Spikenard
Another intensely relaxing oil, spikenard has a sweetly pungent scent that eases restlessness, promotes sleep and is an effective de-stressor. Steam-distilled from the roots of *Nardostachys jatamansi*, a plant that flowers with tiny clusters of white and purple blooms, spikenard can quieten the mind to let your spirituality blossom.

Add 2 drops spikenard oil and a few drops of lavender oil to 1 tablespoon carrier oil. Add to a warm bath at night for a soothing pre-bed ritual.

CROWN CHAKRA SPRAY

Let this luxurious sacred blend clear your crown and soothe your soul.

INGREDIENTS

6 drops lavender essential oil
10 drops juniper essential oil
4 drops myrrh essential oil

50 ml (1¾ fl oz) water

Preparation: 5 mins | **Storage time:** 6 months | **Storage container:** amber spray bottle

To create an aromatic spritzer that soothes and supports the crown chakra, add the oils to the water in a small, portable amber or dark blue spray bottle. To raise its vibrations, drop a few small pieces of amethyst into the bottle as well. To use, spray in the air around your head and inhale deeply.

FOOD

Since the crown chakra is the highest of the spiritual chakras, it is less about fortifying the physical body with food and more about nourishing the mind and the spirit. Many teachers suggest fasting as a way to engage less with our physical needs and more with the universal wisdom of the soul. Working on the crown chakra is also about purification, so certain foods that help the body with detoxification can be helpful for the crown chakra. On an energetic level, foods that are white resonate with the colour of *sahasrara*.

FASTING
Many religious practices include some form of fasting. As with all things associated with this chakra, if you want to fast, do so mindfully.

WHITE DETOXIFYING FOODS

A number of white foods are particularly detoxifying, helping to boost the body's systems and support the crown chakra.

Cauliflower: This cruciferous vegetable contains a component called glucosinolates, a phytonutrient that has been shown to boost the liver's detoxification enzymes, which naturally support the body's detoxification process. Add roasted cauliflower as a side dish, or blend it up in soup (see page 152).

Onions & garlic: While the pungency of onions and garlic is beneficial for the solar plexus chakra, they are also good for the crown chakra thanks to sulphur-containing amino acids that help boost liver function and improve the body's detoxification.

Parsnip: This is a root vegetable that is thought to have detoxifying qualities. It is high in vitamins and minerals that help support kidney and liver function. It is full of vitamin K, which helps protect the liver and also has an anti-inflammatory effect.

Coconut: Containing lots of fibre, coconut is a cleansing food and is high in minerals like manganese. It is also rich in healthy fats and amino acids, which can help regulate blood sugar levels. Incorporate coconut oil into your diet, drink coconut water for hydration or add dried coconut to a variety of dishes.

HERBS & SPICES

These herbs have a calming, soothing effect that's perfect for helping to balance the crown chakra.

Camomile: This gentle herb is made from flowering daisy-like white blossoms and has a wonderfully calming effect on the body, while supporting the digestive system. Camomile is an herbal tea mainstay, and though it is less common than other culinary herbs, you can cook with it as well.

Lavender: Much like lavender oil is a lovely tonic for the crown chakra, the herb itself is also supportive. Use it to make an herbal tea, or get creative with your baking.

CONSIDER VEGANISM

If eating meat, seafood and dairy products is part of your diet, you may want to consider eliminating them, especially as you work on balancing your crown chakra. Once we are awakened to the interconnectedness of life, we often feel better if the food we use to nourish our body doesn't come at the expense or suffering of other living beings. If you do include meat, fish and dairy, try limiting your intake. When possible, choose local, sustainable and organic options.

MOMENT OF GRACE

Another way to incorporate higher consciousness into the physical nourishment of the body is by integrating a mindful mealtime ritual. In addition to simply eating mindfully (page 129), take a breath before you pick up your fork or spoon and enjoy a moment of gratitude. After you have thanked the earth and the people who grew and harvested your food, broaden that gratitude to include the divine and ask that the food you are about to eat be blessed to nourish your body and soul.

COCONUT CAMOMILE TEA

Calm the mind and body to help clear and balance the crown.

INGREDIENTS
1 teaspoon dried camomile leaves
   or flowers
1 teaspoon coconut flakes

Add the camomile and coconut flakes to a small teapot. Fill with 300 ml (10 fl oz) boiling water and allow to steep for about 8 minutes. Pour through a sieve and enjoy.

ROASTED SESAME CAULIFLOWER SOUP

A light, yet satisfying, detoxifying blend.

INGREDIENTS

1 small onion, sliced into wedges

1 small parsnip, sliced

1 small cauliflower, in florets

2 teaspoons olive oil

salt and pepper

1 tablespoon sesame seeds

6 sage leaves

250–300 ml (8½–10 fl oz) boiling
vegetable stock or water

1 tablespoon tahini

juice of ½ lemon

Preheat the oven to 180°C (350°F). Put the onion, parsnip and cauliflower on a baking tray. Drizzle with the olive oil and season with salt and pepper. Roast for 15 minutes. Remove and stir, then add half the sesame seeds and 3 sage leaves. Roast for another 5-6 minutes until the vegetables have softened. Transfer the vegetables to a blender and add the stock and tahini. Leave for 5 minutes to let flavours develop, then blend until smooth. Season with lemon juice and salt and pepper. Add more water to achieve desired consistency. Toast the remaining sesame seeds and sage on a small baking tray for 8 minutes, or until golden brown. Serve the soup, sprinkled with the toasted sesame seeds, leaves and more pepper.

YOGA POSES

Poses that balance the body, stimulate the crown of the head and encourage deep rest are all wonderful ways to support the crown chakra.

PADMASANA (Lotus Pose)

Sit in a straight-legged position. Bend your right knee up and out, rolling your upper thigh out from the hip. Flexing your foot and holding it underneath the ankle, pull your heel in, resting your right foot in the crease of your left thigh. Bend your left knee, rotating your upper left thigh out from the hip. Flex your foot and, holding it underneath your ankle, bring your left foot up and over your right leg, drawing your heel in to your belly and resting your foot in the crease of your right thigh. Press both heels in to your belly to draw your knees closer together and press the outer edges of your feet down to relieve pressure between your shins. Bring your hands to your knees, palms facing up, and bring your index finger and thumb to touch. Lengthen your spine. Stay for five breaths. Unwind and repeat with the opposite leg.

SASANGASANA (Rabbit Pose)

Start from a kneeling position, with your hips on the bottom of your feet. Wrap your hands around your feet, so your thumbs rest on the outside of each foot, fingers on the inside and your palms cover the bottom of each heel. Exhale, lift your hips so your arms straighten and round your spine forward. Roll onto the crown of your head, bringing your forehead towards your knees. (If there is too much pressure on the crown of your head, slide your grip down lower on your feet.) Press the tops of your feet into the mat; soften and relax your shoulders. Stay for five breaths and slowly roll up.

VRIKSHASANA (Tree Pose)

From Mountain Pose (page 34), shift your weight onto your left leg, grounding your foot into the mat. Bend your right knee and, using your right hand on your ankle, bring your right foot up, placing it so the sole of your right foot is pressed against your inner left thigh, near your groin. Press into the sole of your foot with your thigh. Bring your hands into prayer position at the heart centre then raise your arms above your head, hands together. Stay for five breaths. Exhale, lower your arms and bring your leg down. Repeat on the other side.

SIRSASANA (Headstand)

From Child's Pose (page 35), interlace your fingers with your forearms on the floor, palms facing, elbows shoulder-width apart. Nestle the back of your head into your hands, with the crown of your head on the floor. Straighten your legs into Dolphin Pose (page 135). Engaging your core, bend your knees lifting both feet off the floor. Straighten your legs, feet to the ceiling. Keep pressing into your forearms to lift up, relieving any pressure from your neck and crown of the head. Stay for five breaths. Bend your knees and lower your legs back down.

SAVASANA (Corpse Pose)

Lie on your back with your knees bent. Extend your arms to the side, about 45 degrees from the body, palms facing up. Tuck your shoulder blades beneath your back and stretch your legs out one at a time. Close your eyes, relax your face, mouth and jaw. Work your way down your body to your toes. Stay for five minutes. Open your eyes and wiggle your fingers and toes. Bring your arms over your head, roll to your left side, knees to chest. Lean into your hands and come up to seated.

VISUALISATION, MEDITATION & AFFIRMATIONS

FULL BODY TUNE-UP

Lie down or sit in a comfortable position. Close your eyes. Take three deep breaths, inhaling through your nose and exhaling through your mouth. Bring your attention to your root chakra. Visualise a small spinning red sphere where *muladhara* is located. With every breath, send your intention to the sphere, watching it become clear and vibrant. Bring your attention to your sacral chakra, visualising a small spinning orange sphere. Work your way up the body, repeating this visualisation at the solar plexus chakra with a yellow sphere, the heart chakra with a green sphere, the throat chakra with a light blue sphere, and the third eye chakra, with an indigo sphere. When you reach the top of your body, imagine a bright white light beaming through the crown of your head. Breathe the energy of that white light down your spine through every chakra until you reach the root chakra then breathe it back up. When you reach the crown again, voice a crown chakra affirmation that resonates with you. Give thanks and open your eyes.

Sound Meditation

The seed syllable, or *bija* mantra, for *sahasrara* can take on different sounds. Some, like with *ajna*, use 'om' (pronounced 'auummm'). Others use 'ah'. Chant them slowly and repeatedly, letting the sound reverberate at the crown of your head.

AFFIRMATIONS

Bring your awareness to the divine and nurture your inner guide with crown chakra affirmations. Use one of the following suggestions, or let them inspire you to create your own personalised affirmation depending on the energy you need. Say it out loud to your reflection in the mirror in the morning and at night, or at the end of a yoga practice. You can also say it silently, whenever you want or need to.

I am worthy of divine love.
I honour the light within me.
I am open to the wisdom of the universe.
I see the divine in the everyday,
*   and the light within every being.*
I am here, I am present.
I feel true peace.
I know my place in the universe; I feel
*   protected and connected.*
My heart and mind are open; the energy
*   of the universe flows through me.*
I move mindfully, guided by the wisdom
*   of the divine.*

RITUALS & ACTIVITIES

Raising your consciousness may seem like an overwhelming task, but there are actually very simple, everyday ways to open yourself up to the divine and help build your spiritual practice.

Be in the moment. We spend so much of our time thinking about the past or planning for the future. Clearly, it is impossible to live a modern life without doing some of both. But when we are reliving something that's already happened or thinking about something that may occur, we aren't fully living in the moment, and this moment is truly the only one we have. Being mindful, bringing our awareness to our body, appreciating the moment for what it has to offer, whether we are stopping to smell a flower, laughing with a friend or brushing our teeth, is an easy way to see these tiny moments as part of the bigger miracle of life.

Seek out silence. Take the practice of silence that you may have begun while working on the throat chakra and deepen it (page 117), by actively seeking out silence. If you live in an urban area, immersing yourself in real quiet might be a bit of a challenge. Try to find somewhere – whether a park or simply a sacred space in your home – that nourishes you with silence and visit it regularly. Spend some time actively being quiet – by yourself and with others. Make room for your inner wisdom and the spirit to connect.

Return to nature. Just as it nourishes the root chakra, being in nature offers a way to partake in the wonders of this earthly existence while also connecting to the spirit. In fact, simply connecting with nature can look a whole lot like prayer.

Practice prayer. Prayer can mean a number of different things to different people, but what it always aims to do, is to devote energy to thanking the divine and welcoming guidance. Integrate a prayer practice into your daily life, whatever you want that practice to look like. It could mean meditating or chanting. It could mean watching waves crash on a beach and thanking the universe for such gracious and awe-inspiring beauty. However you practise, spend some time every day actively connecting with a power greater than yourself.

Be of service. This is the true essence of the crown chakra and there are myriad ways to do so in your daily life. It can be as simple as opening the door for someone, dropping food off to a friend or checking in with an elderly relative or neighbour. Every day is an opportunity to be of service, in ways both great and small. And each opportunity can open you up to the daily miracle of existence.

INDEX

First published in 2017 by Hachette Livre, Marabout division
58, rue Jean-Bleuzen, 92178 Vanves Cedex, France

This edition published in 2021 by Smith Street Books
Naarm | Melbourne | Australia | smithstreetbooks.com

ISBN: 978-1-92241-7-626

Project manager (for Smith Street Books): Aisling Coughlan
Author: Lisa Butterworth
Recipe author: Amelia Wasiliev
Editor: Kathy Steer
Photographer: Lisa Linder
Stylist: Giovanna Torrico
Cover design: Michelle Mackintosh
Internal design: Michelle Tilly

Printed & bound in China by
C&C Offset Printing Co., Ltd.

Book 199
10 9 8 7 6 5 4 3 2

NOTE: The author has researched each essential oil used in this book but is not responsible for any adverse effects any of the oils may have. All the essential oils are used at your own risk. If in doubt, contact a qualified aromatherapist. When practising the yoga poses, listen to your body and modify where necessary. Inversions (including Plough Pose, Shoulderstand and Headstand) should not be practised during menstruation. Those with asthma should be mindful when practising breathwork.

ACKNOWLEDGEMENTS: My introduction to, and deepening understanding of, the chakra system came through a handful of dear and dedicated yoga teachers – it's been an honour to learn from them on this decades-long journey. Thanks to Catie Ziller for her trust and support, Kathy Steer for her insightful, painless edits and Michelle Tilly for bringing so much of this book to life with her designs and illustrations. Thank you to Amelia Wasiliev for her recipe-writing genius and photographer Lisa Linder for lending this book her incredible talent. And I'm forever grateful for my family and all their good energy that fortifies me daily.